The First 60 Days
A Memorial of Eternal Love and the Grief that Follows

By Donald T. McMahon

© Copyright 2023 by Donald T. McMahon
This is a first edition.
All rights reserved.

No part of this publication may be reproduced, distributed, or transmitted in any form or by any means, including photocopying, recording, or other electronic or mechanical methods, without the prior written permission of the publisher, except as permitted by U.S. copyright law.

The First 60 Days
A Memorial of Eternal Love and the Grief that Follows

By Donald T. McMahon

There will be no memorial for her
Fashioned by the hand of man
No alabaster obelisk, nor polished granite stone
No Taj Mahal, nor gleaming pyramid
With magical words engraved to read
Of a life well lived and loved and accomplished accolades
Not even her name, or birth and death decrees
Laser etched or chiseled in perpetual precision
To remind generations of her footsteps or her breath
Instead, a circle of unhewn, found stones
Placed by her own hands in a quiet field
In a community of cedars and pines and a peach tree
No garlands nor florist arrangements
Instead, grasses and Creator placed wildflowers
A medicine wheel comforting us with directions
East, South, West, North, Above, Below
The guideposts of origins and destinations
The hOMeplace of the ancients and oracles
Commemorating HER life in eternal harmony with All Life
The Angels, ArchAngels, all relations and Christ dance here
Around the Circle, the Wheel within the Wheel
And as the rain washes the stones clean of her ashes
And she feeds the Earth as she fed us all
The Medicine wheel turns as Mother shivers
And Mary watches as the stones dissolve
And all is renewed, and resurrection is made manifest
Her voice is heard in the wind
Her face is seen in the clouds
The plants speak her name
There is no need for man to do anything

Dedication

This book is dedicated to the memory of Pamela Bessent Holder McMahon, a woman who was not famous, but affected the lives of so very many people. She worked in service to anyone in need, quietly, humbly, with no expectation of acknowledgement or gratitude, with the perfect words, or a hug, or a simple, but sumptuous meal. But when she opened her throat and sang, the angels and all the holy hosts would join in, and if you were fortunate enough to be present, all the heavens would stand still and listen.

She was known by some as "Beloved Woman," or "Mother of Many." She was known by her children simply as "Mom," and to her grandchildren as "YaYa." To me, she was my partner, my completion, my heart, the epitome of Love on Earth, and her loss is as devastating as the extinguishing of the sun. I am the unwilling chronicler of an event so brilliant and spectacular that I remain permanently dazed and blinded by being a participant in her life.

It is also dedicated to my family. My children and grandchildren have steadfastly supported me and each other through this period of grief, loss, and learning to live in a new and strange world without her physical presence.

And finally, to our friends, neighbors, and the multitude of readers who have encouraged me, witnessed, and walked with me as this book unfolded, I say "Thank You" and hold you all tightly in my heart.

And So It Is.

Introduction

This is not a normal book. This is the impromptu diary of a man in deep grief and disbelief at his circumstances. It is a true story of a Love that transcends time and life itself and the companion that always walks a step behind in the shadow of great love, waiting to fulfill the contract and is hidden in details, but always guaranteed, grief.

Our life together was always so unique and strange that observers would ask us to describe what we were doing. It led to endless stories and descriptions of how it was possible to exist in the unboxed, unrestrained, full throttle movie that was Pam and Donald T. There were efforts to chronicle what was happening to us, but the words could never seem to catch up with us. By the time we would write a line, our reality had moved on to another chapter and we would abandon the writing task. Neither of us was very good at solidifying life in that way.

To be the one left behind to finally write the story was never an option for either of us. We always believed that when the inevitable end to the fairy tale came that somehow we would join hands and ascend into the pure realm of everlasting Love together....forever. Sometimes things don't work out the way we plan. I think we both knew that it was possible that one of us would leave before the other, but we were hoping to go out in a blaze of glory as One.

So when the dark night came with the cleaver to consummate the "Till Death Us Do Part" of the agreement, it was me who walked out of the hospital while she flew. I became the survivor, the widower, the one who hides in the shadows and weeps.

In an effort to assuage the curiosity and soothe the pain of the thousands of people that loved her and were in shock, I started communicating through, of all things, Facebook. And oddly it gave me a voice and a method to process my personal grief and sadness in a public way that I had not expected. I had no desire to write or be this visible through this process, but it was like I had no choice. What started out as a death announcement turned into a stream of almost daily posts that I could not seem to stop. And whatever I was processing seemed to resonate with readers and even helped them with their own grieving journey.

So this book has no chapters, it has dates. It is the raw, unfiltered, unedited words thoughts and methods of a man dealing with unbearable loss and sorrow as they happened. I hope that readers will find something of value in the convoluted, unusual and beautiful Love story that is the Tale of Pam and Donald T.

Acknowledgements

This book is largely due to the constant encouragement of my family, friends, and the community of readers who held and supported me through this period of intense grief and recollection. Since we were never very good chroniclers, I want to thank those photographers who managed to beautifully capture some fleeting parts of our lives and whose art has given some visual pointers to what lies beneath the words. When I first saw the "Pam With Closed Eyes" portrait by J. Tomas Lopez shortly after her passing it was almost too perfect, and was painful to look at. But then I fell in Love all over again.

Then, as I continued to write with the ambition to make this into a book, he began to grace me with a string of photographs from the last 50 years that are soul capturing…Thank you

There are other fabulous images from our dear friend Steven Ray Miller, Mark Johnson, and others who helped to make us appear real. And those closest friends who called every morning at 6:30 to make certain that I was still here…Thank you.

Mary Ruth Dobbins who pressed us into telling our story over and over and convinced us that we were important, and gave us financial assistance to begin what I finish alone…Thank you.

And to Ms. Charlotte Babb, storyteller, painter and trusted friend whose editorial assistance and guidance through the self-publishing process pushed me to this point…Thank you

To my son Josh and my granddaughter Fiona who designed the cover perfectly. It was Fiona's idea to make the spine red. She looked at me with those ancient, innocent eyes and said, "The spine has to be red. Red is the color of Love." That statement is so deep on so many levels…Thank you.

And lastly, to all those beings named and un-named, seen and un-seen who have assisted in this action…Thank you.

February 23, 2022

This is the hardest thing I've ever had to write. It seems that my dear partner, wife, friend, lover, mother of my children and companion of 56 years passed away this morning at 3:30. Very quick, very unexpected. However it was possible for me and the boys to be there and hold her when she took her last breath. I was hesitant to post anything, but I see that word is leaking out, and I don't want anyone to be hearing bits and pieces. We in our family are so saddened and are feeling totally lost at the moment. We have not been able to talk on the phone because nobody seems to have a voice right now, and so I apologize for sending any texts to anyone. Please send love and blessings. And if anyone wants to honor Pam in any way just go out and do something nice for somebody today. And maybe sing a little song. I love you all. So many people loved her that it is beyond belief. I send my forever Gratitude to everyone who loves her and I will see you soon thanks, Donald T.

I will still be monitoring her channel for some time now. The posts might be different because I'm not her. Donald T.

Feb 25, 2022

I feel like I need to put something out here to let everyone know what's going on. I've seen some people say that it was a heart attack. It was not. It was an undetected aneurysm on the artery behind her heart. I do want to tell you that she lived her life exactly the way she wanted to and finished it exactly the way she wanted to. She was dancing on the rebounder and stepped off to take a sip of water and all of a sudden said "Ouch my chest hurts. I can't breathe," and in two seconds she was gone. She never regained consciousness. And the word from the cardiac people at the hospital was that her heart stopped right at that moment.

I feel like I need to post something here because the wave that is passing through that I see on Facebook is so massive and she affected so many more people than I ever had any idea. I'm gonna do my best to post a little something each day to keep her spirit of living a life of love, and service, and gratitude alive. This is without question the most difficult thing I've ever done in my life. I will try to keep these little postings brief but I do wanna continue it. I can't even keep up with reading the volume of comments and testimonials that are coming through.

It is truly overwhelming but comforting. In the past Pam would read each and every comment and post a heart with it to let you know that she read it. I'm not sure I can do that, the volume is too large. But I'm reading as much as I possibly can each day. Just know that she loved every single one of you out there and I do too. Blessings on this day and all of you, and again, if you wanna do something for her, do an act of kindness and maybe sing a little song and especially do the act of kindness to somebody that you don't like. Thank you.

February 27, 2022

The story begins. Pam was born on July 6, 1945 in Fort Smith, Arkansas. Ten days later on July 16, 1945 the first atomic weapon was detonated, and exactly one month after Pam's birth, August 6, 1945, the first atomic weapon was used on a human population. I don't believe these events were random. One was the birth of genuine Love on earth, the other was the beginning of a spiral into fear and insanity. There is always balance. The opposite of Love is not hate, but fear. Two other births on July 6 are the 14th Dalai Lama, born exactly 10 years earlier, and George W. Bush, born 1 year later. There are plenty of other creative and influential people who share this birth date, but I thought these were particularly interesting.

At the time of her birth, her father was serving in the Army in New Guinea as a field medic. She was 1 year old when he returned. Shortly after his return, he was offered a position with the park service in Columbia, SC to develop a state park in the sandhills area outside of Columbia. The park was named Sesqui Centennial Park and this is where Pam spent the rest of her childhood. It was a 1500-acre park and her family and one other were the only full time residents. Sesqui was a beautiful and peaceful place of white sand, black water lake, pine trees, azaleas, camellias, and other flowering plants. There is a divine feeling in the presence of the pines that whisper comfort with a light breeze and have a fragrance that makes a person feel clean. On our walks Pam would always listen for the sound of the wind in the pines and sniff the air for that pine scent. The park had facilities for swimming, picnicking, hiking, fishing, and a concession stand with a large concrete pavilion for dancing to the jukebox. My family loved to go to Sesqui in the summer to get away from in heat and humidity in Columbia and let my siblings and I swim and enjoy the beauty of the park. This is where OUR story begins.

I was 8 years old. I was on one of those summer visits to the park, when I saw her for the first time. Pam has always been a dancer, and at that time she was using some skates called Rocket Skates, which were a precursor to inline skates. They allowed her to dance like she was wearing ice skates. She was practicing a routine for her dance recital on that concrete dance pavilion and wearing some kind of flowing costume. When I saw her floating across the floor so gracefully, I was overwhelmed. I had never seen anything like this. The only image that seemed to come close to what I was seeing was some of the angel statues in our Catholic church. I recognized her in some way that filled me with awe. I knew her. I hid in the bushes and watched her, afraid to show myself to this vision. I watched her for a long time. Everything else in my 8 year old mind disappeared and I was solely focused on a timeless moment. She didn't see me.

That's all I'm going to write today. I will keep going as I can.

March 4, 2022

I was born March 31, 1945 in Columbia, SC into what could be called a lower middle class family. My father was one of eight Irish Catholic boys. Both my mother and father grew up in difficult times in the Olympia mill village in Columbia. At the end of World War II my father was able to obtain financing for a home in the Eau Claire neighborhood. Life was much simpler then than today, at least in my life. It was possible to ride the city bus pretty much anywhere without fear. The police were always your friend and who you ran to if you got in trouble. Again, at least for me. Two of my father's brothers were police officers and made trusting the police easy. Pam and I grew up and graduated high school without ever going to school with a person of color. Segregation was the law of the South. I'll talk more about these issues later, but this is mostly about our Love story.

My mother was one of three members of a singing trio with her two sisters. They performed all over the South to audiences including returning veterans. They sang tight three-part harmony songs like the Andrews and McGuire Sisters. Think "Mr. Sandman." I began singing on stage with them when I was four years old. I will be forever grateful to my mother and my aunts for giving me the love of singing and performing.

We, along with all the McMahon clan, were faithfully practicing Catholics. We were always at Mass on Sunday, and all the midnight masses and Easter masses. When all my uncles, aunts, and cousins were there, we had our own section of the cathedral. So, my parents sent me to parochial school for my first four years. I was chosen by the nuns to be trained in music, and I was taken out of class every day for classical piano lessons. I spent a great deal of time in church in those years and developed a deep and lasting feeling of spiritual connection with God. Beginning when I was six years old, I began spending many hours in the church alone, looking at the statuary, and REALLY feeling the presence of the Divine.

I know, I'm rambling, but all of this is important later in the story.

Pam and I went to different schools, but I was always aware of her. During high school her boyfriend was from my school, and she said she noticed me because I was a "bad boy." I don't think I was that bad, but because I began drinking alcohol and smoking when I was thirteen, I guess it led to some bad behavior. She was in theater and dance, and I played in different configurations of bands, rock and roll, country, and later jazz and folk.

In 1965 I was in a college production of a play called "Dark of the Moon," and I played the leading role of the Appalachian witch boy who falls in love with a human. We had a large cast and many people were unfamiliar with makeup, and our director reached out to the local community theater for assistance with makeup. Pam volunteered. When she came in the door and our eyes met for the first time, it was absolutely electric. I knew, and she knew.

After rehearsal, she said to me "Do you need a ride home?" I would have said yes even if I had to leave my car there, but as it turns out, I was riding that city bus home that night, so I said "Why yes, I would love a ride." She drove to my parents' house to drop me off, and we began talking. We talked until the sun came up, and we talked for 56 years after that. You would think subject matter would get thin after 56 years. As the sun came up I asked her if she would like to come in and meet my parents and have some breakfast. She felt that it might be awkward for a woman to come in with me at sunrise, but I assured her they were used to it and it would be okay.

From that moment on there was never a time in my life where she was not in my thoughts in some way. So this is what Love feels like.

But there was a problem. She was engaged to someone else, and wedding plans were already underway.

I'll write more soon, and hopefully more concise. So much of this will not follow in chronological order.

March 7, 2022

Ah sweet Love. When we encounter the perfect Love in our lives, we enter a form of time warp. Days and nights become markers for more contact with our Beloved. When Pam and I discovered each other that night in the theater, all else in my life became sidelined, and to this day she is on my mind in some way, each minute. The next six months were a whirlwind of joy. There were not enough days, and not enough time to satisfy the longing for contact. This was young Love at its strongest.

Both Pam and I were still living with our parents, and I was a full-time college student. Pam had returned home from college because she had realized that college life was not in her personal interests and had gone back to teaching tap at Calvert/Brodie Dance Studios. Pam had been a dancer her entire life, and anyone who has been around when there is music playing has seen her begin to sway to the rhythms and move right on into unrestrained dancing.

We began playing music together during that time, and our first group was a five-piece acoustic jazz ensemble. Boy we sounded good. It was also difficult to find an audience in Columbia for our style.

There was no end to our conversations, and I would find every opportunity to continue the relationship. If she had to do laundry and fold clothes, I learned how to fold clothes and talk. But let me be clear, there was no sex. This was a relationship so deep that we couldn't even get around to sex.

I knew in the background, that the wedding plans were continuing to evolve, and I kept asking what she intended to do because we were perfect together. Now, Pam should really tell this part of the story, and there's a way for that, and I will explain later, but for now let me say that she was still young, her fiancé was older, mature, and was well established in a successful career. I was just nineteen years old, living with my parents, and still hitchhiking around a lot. She kept telling me not to worry, that she would take care of it. But it kept getting closer, and every so often, she would go to Philadelphia to meet with him and his parents.

On one such occasion, she returned with an engagement ring on her finger, and my heart sank with a distinct feeling of dread. She was now saying it may be too far gone and she may have to go through with it. She didn't know how to get out. Big wedding plans had been made, bridesmaids dresses ordered, wedding gown ordered, and the dance school was assisting in making it a full scall production.

Finally as the date was drawing very close, I told her she was going to have to make a choice between her fiancé, and me.

She chose him. I was completely devastated, and said that I couldn't stay and watch this, so I packed my guitar and left for New York City. I could stay at my uncle's apartment in the Village and it was truly the best of times in the Village with Bob Dylan and all the folkies on the street.

I buried myself in music and New York street life, and cried a lot. In September she did it. There is a whole story about the wedding which I'll get into next time.

March 12, 2022

I know I left everyone hanging. It's been a rough and wonderful few days. I finally was able to bring her ashes home on Wednesday.

Abandoned. When Pam married "the other guy" in 1966, that's what I felt. I worked in New York as a busboy at a cafe in Central Park during the day, and played music where I could during the night. I was always praying that before the wedding she would miraculously appear, and we would be happy ever after. Didn't happen.

This part of the story should really be told by Pam, and when I get our "project" done, you will be able to listen to her do that. Due to the generosity of a wonderful woman, we have 12 hours of audio and video of Pam and I telling our story. I'll let you know when it's ready.

There are always at least two sides to every story, and here, today, you are getting the story from my perspective. I'm going to tell you this part as best I can from my memory of Pam's description of events.

The Wedding. Pam said that as the time for the wedding approached, she was getting more and more depressed, thinking this was a big mistake. She told her mother and close confidants of her concerns and was met by the old "It's just pre-wedding jitters. It's going to be fine." When she expressed her concerns to her fiancé, his response was that the families had already spent a lot of money in preparations for the wedding, and they were not going to disappoint them. He said that on the wedding day she was going to be walking down that isle, and that if she wanted a divorce afterward, they would work that out then, but she was going to be walking down that isle. She says she felt powerless in that moment and that her life just seemed out of her control. She became a much stronger woman later.

On the day of the wedding, she was crying uncontrollably, and feeling that her life was over.

As she was standing with her father waiting go down the aisle, my dear friend who had been in New York with me over the summer, literally jumped out of the bushes and said "Pam, you can't do this. You are breaking Don's heart and it's wrong. I have a plane ticket for you to New York, just stop and come with me and I'll take you to him." Her father was asking who this young man was, and did he need to call police. Pam assured her father that it was okay, and told my friend that he had to leave, that she was going through with the wedding. In tears and feeling that she was making the biggest mistake of her life, and that basically her life was over, she finally walked down the aisle, said the vows, and was married.

She described to me that she was never happy in that marriage but felt totally helpless and unempowered. I guess this experience would come back to give her the courage and the tools she needed to council and help many, many women to face these challenges and empower themselves later in her life.

She and her husband moved to Bryn Mawr, Pennsylvania in a small apartment near the college campus.

This was in 1966, and she and I, and a great number in my generation, were beginning to feel the weight of the civil rights movement, and the impacts of the war in Vietnam. We were following different paths into the wilderness of insanity that was the '60s.

That's all for now, I'll continue as soon as I am able. I am so happy that people are enjoying my telling our story, and I hope that in the telling it will somehow help others to find their way through this experience we call life. I know it's helping me right now.

March 13, 2022

Now I know we left Pam in an unhappy marriage, and me in New York as an unhappy busboy, but I have to take a short detour to explain some of the historical issues of our times that would affect, and influence our romantic, physical, intellectual, and spiritual lives forever.

One was segregation and the racial tensions of the South in the 1950's and 60's. I know it was going on earlier, but I am only going to relate what I experienced and witnessed that is relevant to our story. There is a great deal more that I would like to write about regarding this, but not on Pam's page, and not in this forum. I don't want to create any issues with anyone regarding CRT, or whatever, because overall this is a love story.

We grew up in a segregated South. There was no official mixing of the races. We went to all white schools all the way through high school. I met my first black student at the University of South Carolina in 1964. Pam attended a rural school that was grades 1 through 12, and her mother was the school secretary. There were separate entrances to stores, movie theaters, and other venues, labeled "White Entrance," and "Colored Entrance." There were separate water fountains with the same labels. Black people were not allowed to eat at any facility where white people ate.

In our parts of town, there were lower, middle, and upper middle-income families who, on the surface, led the "Father Knows Best" and "Leave It To Beaver" lives. There were other parts of town where black people lived in cardboard and tar paper shanties. I was warned never to go into these places. Sometimes I did anyway.

The primary musical venue in those days was the Township Auditorium, where currently popular musical acts would appear while touring. This is where we got to see Elvis, Johnny Cash, and many others. It was very exciting to see live music in that way. There was a "Colored Entrance" for the Township, that led to the third balcony. I know because I spent many an evening in that third balcony.

During the early 60's, there was the Chitlin Circuit that had a lot of the black musicians that you didn't always hear on the radio unless you listened to WOIC. I wanted to see them because I was attracted to their music. Something about it made me feel really good, and the rhythms were unbelievable. The only way for whites to attend the Chitlin Circuit shows was to go through the "Colored Entrance." For these shows only, black people were allowed in the regular sections, and any wayward whites were relegated to the third balcony. At these shows there were only a handful of white people in attendance. I always saw Pam there, although we didn't talk or have any contact, but she was consistently one of the few whites there. Shows like BB King, Albert King, James Brown, Bobby "Blue" Bland, Ray Charles, and so many others. Holy Smokes, I had never seen anything like that. The way the people in the audience danced. What?? Can you do that in public? God, I learned so much from those performances. And Pam was always nearby.

In 1962 I started to hear Bob Dylan, Peter, Paul and Mary, and "protest" music in the folk genre. It stimulated something in me that was new. I was starting to be intellectually curious and see that much the world was quite different than my corner. I heard lyrics like "How many times must a man look up before he can see the sky? How many ears must one man have before he can hear people cry?" I was beginning to wake up. I could see Martin Luther King, Jr. and the other marchers walking to obtain voting rights. I began to participate in some of these protests. This was happening for Pam as well.

The number two big issue that was happening was the ramping up of the Vietnam War. Young love was sprouting in a time of darkness. We were growing together in ways that we did not understand at the time.

I'm going to stop now, and I will continue with the Vietnam story next time before I get back to the continuation of our story.

Thank you for listening, and I really appreciate the feedback that I receive from your comments. Even though I don't always respond to them directly, I am always listening to you.

Donald T. McMahon

March 15, 2022

It's been a busy few days since I posted about segregation and racism. The second big dog in the room during this period was the creeping awareness of the war in Vietnam.

I come from a long line of patriotic Irish American warriors. Always first in line to volunteer for service to America and our neighbors. My uncle Paul, the youngest of the eight boys in my father's family, lied about his age, and became a crewman on B-17's and B-29's during the campaign in Europe. He participated in some of the most intense air missions of World War II, being shot down several times. The last time his plane was shot down, he was a lone survivor. The other crewmen were shot as they parachuted down. Paul managed to land in the middle of a German military parade ground and was captured instead of killed. He was the youngest returning prisoner of war from that conflict. He was freed by Russian troops. He was entirely grey at 19 and remained so for the rest of his life. He will become even more involved in the story soon.

As word of the conflict in Vietnam began to circulate, my family, and many others were firmly supportive of our president's position that placed us in Southeast Asia, thinking the "domino effect" of spreading communism would eventually engulf the world if we didn't stop it there. Actually, it was much more complicated, but patriotism is a powerful force.

As I began to spread my wings with trips to New York, and a summer job as a counselor at a camp for handicapped children in Chappaqua, NY, just north of the city, I became exposed to other viewpoints on the war. More research into this conflict began to create doubts in my mind about whether the official position of our government was accurate. I began playing as a regular house musician at a coffee house in Columbia called the UFO. It was a place of really good music, and a safe place to exchange information that was not readily available from daily news, and conversations with my family. The UFO was one of a group of coffee houses that were started in cities where military training was going on. Columbia was the home of Fort Jackson, one of the largest military training facilities in the United States. As part of their function, they offered counseling on how to resist the military draft, and how to get out of the Army if you had conscientious objections to the war. I was still very confused. It was difficult to fully discern which story lines were true.

My high school was extremely patriotic, and Pam's school was just outside of Fort Jackson, so many of the students were from military families and deeply involved in the war effort. Many of my high school classmates volunteered for service as soon as they graduated, some even leaving school early to join up. It was difficult to accept when some of them began to come back injured, or worse, in flag draped coffins. Here I was, beginning to participate in anti-war protest marches, and playing songs of love and peace, all the while dreading the overhanging threat of being drafted myself. I talked with numerous young men who had been drafted and had deep concerns about their service.

It was also during this period that I witnessed both military police, and municipal police come into the coffee house and without warning, just grab people up, who were doing nothing wrong other than openly questioning whether America's participation in the Vietnam conflict was justified. I began to see the police, who I had always trusted as a safe harbor, doing things that were just plain wrong. There were unprovoked beatings and harassment, "up against the wall" moments, and more. This was getting crazier by the minute, and Pam was gone, happily married as far as I knew. We had zero communication during this period. I, like many others, was frightened by what I was seeing. My family was not impressed by my views on the war, or my views about civil rights, and integration. These things were beginning to shred my family and old friends and sew mistrust and division among us all. We were forming camps of thought. Separation and alienation were becoming the norm, and Anger....so much Anger. I was hurt by my loss of Pam, and everything just seemed to cause the pain to get worse. My trust in my country, my family, my friends, my God was all gone. It was dark, and I thought the end was surely near.

Then a light came. Pam called me on the phone and said she was leaving her husband, and asked if I would pick her up at the airport.

I didn't trust her either, but Love, always Love made me say Yes.

Thanks for listening, I'll write more as soon as I can.

March 17, 2022

We left this story with a call from Pam that she was leaving her husband and asking me if I would pick her up at the airport. It's important that I convey what she was doing during her marriage and the plan for escape. I believe these days are the real beginnings of her personal empowerment and gathering strength. I want to remind everyone that there are parts of our story that are only hers to tell, but I will do the best I can from her voice in my memory.

She told me that the family she married into were social drinkers. Social in the form of Bloody Mary's in the morning, lunch cocktails, and gradually working up to Scotch in the evenings. She began to drink heavily, all the while becoming more depressed. Her mother-in-law noticed her depression and sent her to her doctor who prescribed a mild anti-depressant medication, which she began to take, along with the continued alcohol use. It was not a beneficial lifestyle. She said that the apartment was small, and cleaning only took a short time, and then there was nothing to do. She was used to daily dance classes, and she taught tap for fifteen years prior to marriage. She was sinking into a miserable personal darkness. She managed to get a job as a volunteer candy striper at the local hospital. She was always seeking to help others, even when she couldn't seem to help herself. In some ways this was a primary factor in her personality.

After a short while, they offered her a paying job administering EKG's. She enjoyed working at the hospital and began to make some friends outside of her marriage. Another young female co-worker became especially close, and Pam began to frequently meet with her, gradually being introduced to her boyfriend who was a pot dealer. This is when Pam began to trade alcohol for marijuana for her consolation drug of choice. Pot seemed to open her mind to new experiences, while alcohol just took her down the same depressing hole.

She began to go out to the Main Point Coffee House to see performers like Gordon Lightfoot, Phil Ochs, a very young Janis Ian, and many others. Again, music always is leading us in parallel lives toward a new awareness and hope. She began to form in her mind an escape plan. There came a time when her husband needed to travel to Florida on a business trip and wanted Pam to come along. She could stay with some of his family on the coast while he was traveling.

This was the opening she had been looking for. While he was gone for several days, she told his family that she received a call that her father was ill, and she needed to go home immediately. Of course, he was not ill, and she had no idea of where she would stay, and that she would NOT tell her family she was in Columbia or that she had left her husband. She was just taking the big leap of faith that something would happen.

This is when she called me, and I said yes. Oh God, what a joyous, highly charged emotional reunion that was! We went straight from the airport to the coffee house where I was performing, and almost like a stopped moment in time, she came right up on stage with me and began to sing. The harmonies that I always heard in my head began to be present again and music flowed effortlessly.

It carried us to a place in our minds where she wasn't married, the war wasn't happening, and everyone loved each other. Everything was so beautiful. We didn't know how this was going to work out, but we really knew it was good right then. Those were wonderful days of all consuming Love. Pretending there was no husband, and that all was right with the world.

As it turned out, that first night was also the night that Esquire Magazine sent a reporter to cover the coffee house scene, and the effect that the anti-war, resist the draft movement was having in America. They interviewed Pam and me and of course, enjoyed the music that we were making. After that article came out, things changed quickly. I lost my student deferment, became classified as 1A, received a notice to report for a physical, and got a draft notice all within thirty days. And her husband showed up wanting to know what was happening, and not in a good mood.

Things went from bright light and Love to the horrific reality that was 1968.

March 19, 2022

I have draft notice to be inducted into military service, and Pam's husband shows up. We had a couple of weeks of fantasy relationship before it began to crumble. I want to emphasize here that there was still NO sex between Pam and I. I don't know why that's important, but it is. I think this was the most intense Love affair without physical union of all times. Oh, it wasn't because I didn't want to, or have some higher purpose, it was just because it was too fast and personal to risk the change that sex brings into a relationship.

She was staying with some friends from the theater, and I was still living at home with my parents, so we just got together all day and night until I had to go home and rest. I don't know how her husband found her, but he did, and showed up confused and angry.

Pam and I were still spending every day together as much as possible, but now he was in on most of our meetings, and he would come to the coffee house each night to talk with Pam. He was actually a really nice guy. We were friendly and their conversations were never violent or even heavily angry. He was hurt, and in the beginning, he didn't understand why she was leaving him, but in a relatively brief amount of time he understood that she was serious in wanting a divorce, and he agreed.

She said she didn't want anything from the marriage, but he said that she was going to have to come the Pennsylvania and help him explain this to his parents and take half of the stuff in the apartment. She told him she would not go back to Pennsylvania unless I went along as well. He said that would be fine, and so began one of the weirdest journeys of my life.

I had about 30 days before my actual induction date, and I wanted/needed to go to New York to see and seek council from a couple of my mentors to help me with the confusion in my mind of both my looming military service, and the craziness of my Love life and relationship situation. I will talk more about my mentors a little later. Since I needed to go to New York, and she wouldn't go to Philly without me, we decided that I would ride with them to Philly and stay until she was comfortable that the marital split was firmly in place, and then they would give me a ride to New York.

Talk about a strange situation. I was pretty uncomfortable being in the car with Pam and her husband on this wild ride to divorce land. These were the days before easy interstate highway trips to New York, and most of the trip was on the old trusty Highway 1 and other "small" roads. As we traveled, her husband was driving, and Pam was in the passenger seat, with me in the back. Most of the way, Pam and I were "secretly" holding hands beside her seat. Just feeling the skin-to-skin contact was electric enough to keep us soaring in the midst of the drama.

As the day began to fade into twilight, we approached Richmond, Virginia. We could see something was drastically wrong. There were police barricades everywhere, the main roads were blocked, cars were burning as well as some buildings on fire. Tires were burning in the streets, we were hearing gunfire, and the skyline was red. The world was coming apart as Pam, her husband, and I sat in horror, blocked from traveling any further, in what appeared to be a war zone in full conflict. The date was April 4, 1968, and

Martin Luther King, Jr. had just been assassinated. WHAT WAS HAPPENING? Everything was collapsing around us. We couldn't go on, and we couldn't go back. We managed to get a motel room, to get out of the fray, and have at least some sense of refuge.

Talk about weird. Pam, her husband and myself spending the night in a motel room together. There was no sleep to be had because we just watched news coverage, and periodically peeked out through the curtains at the devastation going on outside the motel window. It seemed like Armageddon was happening in all aspects of our lives. Her marriage, my military induction, and the apparent collapse of civil society.

The night was long, frightening, and very uncomfortable on many, many levels to say the least.

By daybreak some sense of order had been restored, and we were able to cautiously continue on to Bryn Mawr to their apartment. In the morning her husband went to work, and we stayed home and contacted a lawyer to begin the actual process of divorce. I stayed with them for a few days while the legal proceedings began to roll on.

When I was sure Pam was safe, and the divorce was firmly under way, with no chance of either of them backing out, I asked them to take me to New York. We soon left on a sunny April day to see my Uncle Paul, and Betty Butterworth, two of the most important people and guiding lights of my life, for counsel. They deserve more than a chapter, so I will talk more about them next time.

We were in Butterworth's apartment, playing music, and Pam was singing those harmonies that we all remember, and there was a level of magic in the air. The music between us was just so good. As they began to leave to return to Philly, and were walking out, Butterworth wanted to talk to Pam in private. Now they had never met before that day, but Butterworth took Pam aside and said "I can see that you and Donny are in Love, but what are you going to do with the husband?" Pam told her that she was getting divorced. Butterworth asked her where she was going to go and what was she going to do, and Pam said "I don't know, but I'm not going home to Columbia, and I'm not staying in Philly."

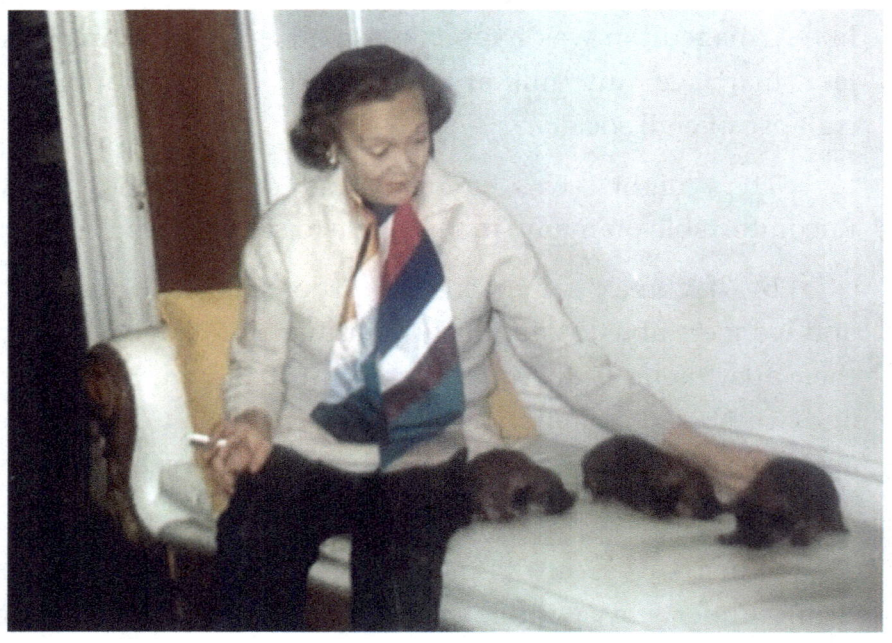

Butterworth said "I Love Donny, and I can see that you Love Donny. Why don't you come here and stay with me until you get on your feet?" Pam was flabbergasted at the outpouring of support from someone she had never met before. Butterworth told her to give her about a week to get some space cleared out in the tiny four flight walk up apartment, and then come on back. Pam agreed and in about a week, her husband delivered her to Butterworth's apartment, gave her a hundred dollars and told her to have a good life.

I in the meantime had reported for induction, was sent to Fort Polk, Louisiana for basic training. Head shaved, in fatigues, already tired from sleep deprivation, and primed for brain washing.

March 20, 2022

The last two days have been difficult emotionally. I don't know why particularly; it must have something to do with the full moon. I thought I was further along on this new solo journey, but the gravity waves of emotion just keep coming. My son Buddy tells me that this is part of the repayment of the loan of Pam and the balance of a great Love.

A rogue wave came up yesterday and chased me from my comfort zone on the beach and washed away my cooler and picnic supplies, leaving me with a clean beach, calm ocean, and a feeling of wtf and that sinking feeling of loss and loneliness. Thankful for my family and the beautiful support that I feel from all of you.

In May 1968 Pam moved in with Butterworth in the tiny apartment on W 53rd Street in NY. Pam was always willing to work and was now becoming much more clever and gaining wisdom and personal strength from Butterworth, just like I did. Within the first week, she had a job as a runway model for a fur dealer. Think everything from rabbit to lynx belly fur coats. I know, she would be horrified by that later, but at the time it was work, empowering and enabling her to stand firmly on her feet and go forward with her life as a divorcee. Since I was in basic training, there was little to no communication between us at that time.

I was going to write about Uncle Paul and Butterworth, but it is beginning to turn into a long story, so I'm going to only hit some of the more important moments. I will write a much longer version for a book. Pam and I started the book years ago and there are a lot of audio files for me to sort through and create a final product.

She was also burning her candle from both ends, and her apartment had become home to several gay men from our hometown theater group who were trying to make it in NY. At Christmas, I got a short leave from the Army, and went to see her in NY. It was immediately evident that we were now living in two different worlds. She was super busy, and very active in the anti-war movement, and I had been significantly brain washed into a soldier mindset. By the way, the American military machine is VERY good at training and modifying behavior. When I left her in NY that Christmas, I had that same sinking feeling that I was losing her that I had during her engagement before marriage. Long distance relationships are difficult.

When I finished one of my trainings, and we were going to receive our deployment orders, I was pretty sure I was alright because nobody from that unit had been given Vietnam duty in a long time. Mostly they got assignments in Germany or Japan.

Out of the 250 men in my company I was the only one to receive orders for Vietnam. And not only that, but my orders were to report immediately, with no leave time. I was to begin processing to leave that day. From that time until I arrived in Oakland, CA processing station, I had an "escort" to make certain that the paperwork was all in order and that I actually arrived without going AWOL. I had time to call both my parents, and Pam and let them know that I was underway for deployment in Vietnam.

When I arrived at the Oakland processing facility, we were kept in a large warehouse type of structure, that covered several city blocks. The doors were kept closed at all times, and there were endless rows of bunks with islands of vending machines scattered out through the building, and loudspeakers that announced frequently the rosters for departing flights. Three times a day we were marched to the mess hall for regular meals, but always with "escorts."

When it was my time to leave, there was a bus with bars on the windows that loaded us right from the door and delivered us to the tarmac for entry to the plane. The next time I deboarded was at Ton Son Nhut airbase at Saigon. Then on to Long Binh for processing and assignment to my unit for the rest of my deployment. I remember getting off the plane at 3 in the morning and the air was thick, hot, and smelled of mildew and diesel fuel. It was the end of the rainy season.

After a day or two of processing, I was waiting for final orders, and my mail that I had not received for days finally caught up to me. There were warning sirens, and we were ordered into a sandbag bunker. There was gunfire and mortar explosions nearby and I realized I was not in Kansas anymore, and I was in a messed up spot.

At least the mail was here, and there was a letter from Pam. I opened it and as I read it, all the light in me left and darkness and anger and fear began to replace any feelings of happiness or hope that I had left. In essence the letter from Pam was a "Dear John" letter informing me that she was now living with another guy in New York, and never wanted to see or hear from me again. Abandoned for the second time.

That moment was the worst moment of my life, my dark night of the soul, until February 22, 2022 when her Spirit departed her physical body

Donald T. McMahon

March 22, 2022

Now you know what was happening to me, and it's time to talk about what was happening to Pam during my time in the Army and time in Vietnam. I am relating this the best I can as I remember her talking about it.

Butterworth...I really can't go on with this part of the story without at least some explanation of Butterworth. As I began to spend more time in NYC with my Uncle Paul in 1964-65, it was a wild time. He was a single, handsome, talented man with a penchant for the dramatic. He spent a lot of time with the creative, wealthy elite in the city, and friends from all over the world.

He took me under his wing and began to show me a whole different side of life than my sheltered upbringing in suburban Columbia could ever imagine. We drank in bars with celebrities, went to Broadway and off Broadway shows, and partied with the rich and famous. He knew people in the art world, the music world, the theater world, the business world, and even interesting characters of European royalty.

The parties were wild. At one party I noticed a woman completely unlike any of the others at these gatherings, and in fact, not like anyone I had ever met. She was in her late 50's or early 60's at that time and had a masculine/feminine look that was unique. She wore trousers and a nice shirt with the collar turned up in the back, and always an ascot or scarf around her neck. She had a tanned weathered appearance, heavily wrinkled and obviously a person of the outdoors, unlike any of the others at this party, which were richly dressed, powdered and painted, and trying to impress everyone in the room.

I was drawn to her and approached her and began a conversation. I was only 18 at the time and quite innocent, but I could drink. She talked of fishing, and animals, and sailing in such a captivating way, all the while drinking vodka neat, smoking one cigarette after another, and speaking with such a delightful British accent. She liked my music.

Most of the people at the party just wandered by as I played or gave polite applause while never interrupting their constant conversations, but she sat and intently watched me play, and really listened to the lyrics. Over the next few years, she became such an inspiration in my life. I visited her regularly in her apartment and sang and talked of so many things.

She and her sister had grown up in the home of a publishing family in London, and knew so many famous writers, and musicians and artists. She knew Dylan Thomas, and spent time in Paris listening to Django Rhinehart, and the Paris music scene in the 1930's. Oh gosh, I could go on and on about her life, but that's really a completely different story. She introduced me to a world so far beyond any books or movies, that I always rushed straight to her apartment every time I arrived in the city. She was such a wonderful, generous person.

When she listened to Pam and I that day, she was captivated by the music, and Pam's harmonies and she just sat quietly listening and watching. Her invitation for Pam to stay with her caught me completely by surprise.

On her first day with her, she introduced Pam to a contact that led to the modelling job and put Pam very quickly on her feet. I don't think Pam stayed with her more than a few weeks, but they really loved each other.

After Pam moved into her own apartment on 17th Street, she really got busy with modelling, and the music/dancing gig at Your Father's Mustache, and if that wasn't enough, she also crocheted dresses that she sold to a boutique in the Village. She was keeping busy. I can see in retrospect how there was really no room for our long-distance relationship, and it gradually faded away.

Not long after I was deployed, her brother was also deployed, and a close friend who had played with her and her brother in their first musical group. So she had three loved ones in Vietnam at the same time. She began to get depressed, eventually leading to a call to the suicide hotline where they told her that there were so many suicidal people in NY that they could get her an appointment in three weeks. She began laughing and told them that if she was still alive in three weeks that she sure wouldn't need them.

She was really despondent, and while wandering the streets, she came across a group of Hari Krishna's chanting in the park. She just started chanting with them, and eventually they asked her to join them for a meal. She went with them, had a good meal, and began meeting them on a regular basis for chanting. She said they were so kind, and never pressed her to join their movement in any way. They just gave her Love, food, and a will to live. She eventually did move out of her apartment and into the apartment of a fellow musician, and they began a brief romantic relationship.

That is when she sent me the letter. She told me later that she never stopped loving me, but that the thoughts of me and her loved ones in the war were too much, and she sort of dissociated to protect herself and keep from taking her own life. I'm so sorry for the grief that my choice to allow myself to be sent to Vietnam caused her and my family. It took me a long time to realize that they suffered just like I did, and possibly more because there was nothing they could do to protect me.

Pam became even more involved with the anti-war movement, and participated in the big march on Washington, where she experienced firsthand the gassing and brutality of the police against protesters. She used her fear for our safety to fuel more involvement in feminism, anti-war, civil rights, and just causes. I in the meantime was just trying to stay alive and getting angrier by the day.

Angry at Pam for abandoning me again, angry at my country for putting me in that horrible position, angry at my parents and friends for allowing this to go on, angry at God for forsaking me. Just ANGRY! As Pam would say later, "Anger is the stepchild of Fear." I was also more frightened than I had ever been, and anger was just a way to placate it for a time. In February 1970, I came home...sort of.

March 24, 2022

There are a couple of more things to say about my time in Vietnam before we go on. When Woodstock happened, I was in Vietnam, and didn't even know it was happening. When a man first walked on the moon I sat on a pile of sandbags and cursed the moon asking God why we were doing that when we were also doing this. When Ho Chi Minh died, I noticed that EVERY SINGLE Vietnamese person was wearing a black arm band in mourning for his passing. Now, he was the leader of the opposing army. I had a clear realization that I was in the wrong place, and we had no business being there. I heard President Nixon say unequivocally that we were not bombing in Cambodia, but I was witness to it.

***

And then, sometime near Christmas 1969, I came into this little "club" we had in Cu Chi where we could get a beer and see a little tiny black and white TV. The Ed Sullivan show came on with musical guest Sly and the Family Stone, and who should I see but Pam, dancing and singing with the Your Father's Mustache band as the opening act. At that moment all the anger that had been building for nearly a year while I was there turned into an ugly hatred, and not just for her, but for the lying of our leaders, the unjustness of the war, and the general lack of integrity of America. I had become radicalized without realizing it.

As my flight lifted from Vietnam there was this overwhelming feeling of relief that I might still get out of this unhurt. Not so. We were all wounded in one way or another. When we landed in Oakland, there were protesters there calling us "baby killers," throwing things and spitting. Mostly from behind plywood barriers, but unmistakably there.

As it turned out, I had more leave built up than remaining active-duty time, so I was being released from active service as well as returning from duty. By the time I was processed out, counting the time from Vietnam, I had not slept in five days. It was near the end of the day, and the person processing my final pay and release orders said I could stay on base until tomorrow or leave base now. I chose the leave now option.

My intention was to get to the first motel and sleep for a couple of days, then go visit some friends in San Francisco. I got on the first city bus away from the processing station. Unfortunately, I fell asleep on the bus. I was awakened roughly by the bus driver shaking me and yelling at me that I was not going to sleep on his bus, and that this was the end of the route and if I wanted to ride further, I would have pay an additional fare. I was totally disoriented. I couldn't have been asleep for more than 30 or 45 minutes. That's when I looked around and realized I had been robbed. My duffle bag and belongings were all gone. All I had was my release orders, and $2500 dollars in new bills that were my final pay.

I asked where we were, and he told me we were at the Oakland International Airport. I got up and left the bus and went into the terminal. I went to the Delta Airlines desk and asked if there was a flight to Columbia, SC and they said yes but boarding would not be for a couple of hours.

I told them I was a returning vet, and I hadn't slept in 5 days, and I would not be able to stay awake for a couple more hours. They offered me the first kindness in a long time. They said, "It's OK son, we'll take care of you." They led me out to the tarmac where the plane was being cleaned and fueled and let me onboard. They put me in a first-class seat while the cleaning crew was working, and asked if there was anything they could do for me. I told them they could bring me a couple of Scotch drinks, which they did, and I woke up in Atlanta in the same plane, taking off for Columbia.

I landed in Columbia at sunrise, and my parents were waiting to take me to breakfast at a pancake house and begin the next phase of my life.

While I was in the Army, my parents sold my childhood home. It was really about "white flight." Someone in my neighborhood had sold their house to a black family, and very quickly almost everyone in the neighborhood, including my parents, had sold their homes.

I don't know what happened to all of my things, but when I arrived "home," there were none of my childhood belongings there, and my parents were living in the upstairs apartment of a funeral home. You had to walk through the funeral parlor to get to the stairs to go up to the apartment. There were often bodies lying in their coffins waiting for the funeral the next day.

By the time I was welcomed home, I had no home, and I had a case a day beer habit, and smoked three packs of cigarettes a day. I only smoked Pall Malls, and Camels, no filtered crap for me.

My parents tried to get me back to some friends, so they called up some of my childhood friends to come take me out. Well, that was a bust. We no longer had a common language, or common interests.

The First 60 Days

I went to see my old theater group thinking that I might resume my theatre training, but their conversations seemed petty, and they had no real awareness of the realities of my experience now.

I tried to go see a band play where I knew some of the band members but it was too early in the afternoon to meet them, so I went to a local bar to keep my beer maintenance up. As I sat at the bar, the TV was showing scenes of the war, and a bearded, guy down the bar from me said, "You just get back?" I said "yes," and he said he had taken that trip, and could he buy me a beer. He became one of the best friends I had in my life. His experiences in Nam were much, much worse than mine I would discover, and he would later become a 20-year crack addict.

Another high school friend who had returned from his Marine service called me up, and we took my father's camper on a trip to the beach. I don't think I can accurately describe how far away mentally I had become from the person who lived here before. I kept thinking that if I could just get to the beach, put my feet in the water, and touch the sand, that I would be OK. We went to Hunting Island State Park on the coast of SC.

That was still in February, and no one is at the beach in February. As we drove in along the beachfront road, I could see the ocean. There were cabins there, but nobody was there. I pulled into the first driveway that I could and hopped out and rushed out to the beach. I could feel the ocean and the sand beneath my feet and I thought I was home.

Then an officer came up and asked if that was my truck, and I answered yes. Then he asked if that was my house, and I said no. He then proceeded to tell me that I needed to get in my truck and get moving. I tried to explain that I was a returning vet, and just needed to get my feet on the ground, but he wasn't listening. He said that if I didn't leave immediately, I would be taken to jail. I think that's when the anger fully matured into rage. I thought to myself, "So this is what America has become, private property and abusive behavior. OK, I'll leave, but I'll be back and bring the war here so you people will know what's actually going on!!!!!"

I'm sure I didn't let my friend who was with me know all that was going on in my head. Now I was getting dangerous and about to boil over. These were all private thoughts. I was going inward...way inward.

At about that time, my Uncle Paul called and said that a private jet was coming to Darlington, SC, and there would be a seat on the returning flight to NYC, and he would like me to come to NY to welcome me home. It was a little 4 passenger Lear jet and scotch whiskey flowed freely.

The little plane landed in NY, and there was a limo waiting on the tarmac to pick me up. Over the next week there was a lot of drinking, partying, and slapping on the back, and welcoming home. But I was messed up. I was still finding myself asleep under the bed sometimes, and diving to the side of the sidewalk when a car backfired, and very nervous and jumpy.

The excessive drinking was not helping. I went to see Butterworth, and while I was there, Pam arrived! #@%. I wanted to kill her, but I Loved her. We had mad sex right there on the floor of Butterworth's apartment, and she moved out of the other guy's apartment and in with Butterworth the next day. She said she had never stopped loving me and all she wanted was to get back together. In my mind I was thinking that if I ever get her alone, I'm going to kill her, for real.

One night Paul took me to a bar where we were drinking Absinthe. That did it. My rage was unleashed. I went crazy. I went to Butterworth's and grabbed Pam roughly and literally dragged her down four flights of stairs, crying uncontrollably, and screaming. I dragged her out in the street where someone tried to stop me, and I threw them down and continued to drag her up the street. This was probably 2 in the morning.

At some point she started to walk with me and try to console me, so the dragging stopped, and the walking began. We walked up and down the entire length of Manhattan until sunrise. As the sun came up, I said, "I'm in deep trouble, and I have to leave the city to try and find some kind of peace within myself." I went straight to the airport and got a plane back to South Carolina.

I moved into a little tent in the forest by myself. I spent some time trying to calm the rage, but all I wanted to do was wake everyone up to the horror. I started a plan to bring violence home. Now I was becoming very dangerous. I had weapons, and I knew how to use them. It was several weeks before Pam got there, and my desire to kill her and a lot of other people was only growing. I was spinning way out of control and couldn't seem to get any hold on a sane reality. The VA was no help.

By the time Pam got there, I was back at my parents' apartment, and my plans were maturing. It was almost time.

Donald T. McMahon

March 25, 2022

Pam arrived in Columbia sometime in late April. She had become a vegetarian and had shaved her head. While I was living in a tent in the woods trying to find some kind of new understanding of God and what was happening to me, she was getting further into activism in NY while preparing to find me again.

She attended the first Earth Day in NYC with a friend and took LSD to wander around the streets and exhibits. It was a warm day, and they found a movie theater that had air conditioning and was participating in Earth Day, so it was free admission. It turned out that what they were showing in the venue was a movie about slaughterhouses. It was very graphic.

I don't know who out there has experience with LSD, but watching a movie about slaughterhouses while tripping can be both horrifying and enlightening. From that moment on, she became a vegetarian. She said she realized the truth about "You are what you eat." For the rest of her life, she would be heavily affected by that experience. That was also the catalyst that finally launched her to Columbia.

There were no plans, just get to Columbia and find me. She had very little money and basically came into Columbia completely broke, financially having spent her money on plane fare. There had been no communication since my meltdown in NY and sudden departure. She had no idea where I was, no money, just a deep knowing that she had to find me.

She contacted some friends from NY that were in Columbia. They were a mixed-race couple, and the man was a black man who had been drafted, and his white wife and beautiful mocha child and they were living in a small mobile home park near Fort Jackson. A mixed-race couple was extremely unusual in South Carolina in 1970 so there was considerable tension around them in the mobile home park. They let Pam stay with them while she tried to find me.

It really wasn't difficult, because I had moved back in with my parents in the funeral home apartment and was busy drinking and smoking myself into a stupor most days. She had no transportation, but she called my parents and got me on the phone. She told me where she was and really needed to see me. She said she had left NY and only wanted to be with me whatever it took. I had bought an old Chevrolet with some of my separation money and had my own plans in motion so I went to the little trailer where we grabbed each other so tightly, not knowing anything other than that moment.

The feeling was beyond description and seemed to move us into another dimension, past all the worries, fears, and held resentments and into a space that had to be Divine Love. Nothing else mattered in that moment except the physical, emotional, and spiritual contact that we felt. Sex, sex, sex, and more sex.

Physical attraction had always been a great driving force in our relationship, although we never actually had a sexual relationship until her divorce was under way. Something about respect and remnants of Catholic guilt, shame, and not wanting to offend God, whatever my perception of Creator. But when we finally did begin to have a physical relationship, it became hot, intense, and completely all consuming.

I'm guessing that our children's souls were beginning to circle around in the Spirit world looking for the opportunity to join us. We couldn't be in the same space without touching, holding, caressing, feeling the perfectness of human sexuality. It is a supremely motivating factor that kind of transcends a lot of the day-to-day issues like eating, getting work, going to the store, or being apart in any way.

Oh, I still had this inner hatred of Pam that was temporarily hidden by the wonder of our reunion. We had absolutely no idea of what we were going to do, but whatever it was, from now on, it was going to be together. In my deepest mind, it meant murder/suicide. I know, that's a scary term and I had to think very hard before I wrote that down, but it was what was actually going on in my head.

Things were so screwed up in the world, and life for me had become a twisted, distorted scene that no longer had much hope in it. Even though what was right in front of me was beautiful and sweet, there was this nagging notion that it was all temporary and at any moment some other tragic event would bring it to a close. I couldn't see the light from wherever I was in my head.

There was no real possibility of resolving all the pain, guilt, and feelings of abandonment except a quick merciful end to it all. Somewhere about here, one of our close friends returned from Nam and was still strung out on heroin. He had been smoking it on cigarettes, and didn't realize he could develop an addiction by just smoking....but you can. He was suffering from the same type of what we would later refer to as PTSD that I was, and he was living in a makeshift shelter under the sea vegetation at the far end of Isle Of Palms, SC. In those days, there were no people or development that far up on the island.

He had a little tent shelter hidden in the bushes, and unless you really knew what you were looking for, you would have no idea that someone was living there. We were good at being invisible. The VA was no help. He did his own withdrawal on his own terms there on the beach. It was truly quite comfortable. A little fire pit, sleeping area, and quiet isolation with only the ocean and sea birds for company. While we were visiting him, we decided to go into town to a movie to get out of the heat and mosquitos for a little bit. The movie was MASH. Probably not the best choice for returning veterans with suicidal tendencies, but we had no idea what the movie was about. Sadly, much later that friend would take his own life, with drugs from the VA.

Did I say we were doing a lot of drugs?? It was mostly marijuana, alcohol, and some anti-depressants, but I had also been introduced to Opium in Vietnam in the form of opiated hashish. I had bought a kilo a month or so before I came back from Vietnam. I liked the dreamy, pastel, colorful experience and lack of pain. I never graduated to heroin like some of my friends, and for that I am eternally grateful.

Pam needed some kind of transportation. When she came with me to my parents' apartment, she noticed a for sale sign on a 1957 Cadillac hearse in the parking lot. She asked about it, and the funeral home owner said he was selling it for $250. Pam wanted that hearse, so I bought it for her. She said she would pay me back.

She dressed that machine up, with beautiful interior painting and curtains, and the back was just the right size for a double mattress with a single mattress across the top. When we were telling these stories to people at spiritual conferences, she would freak older ladies out by referring to her vehicle as a "pussy wagon" She moved into Talbert, which was the vehicle's name. Shortly afterward, I would move into Talbert with her. Believe it or not, those were really wonderful carefree days with no objectives other than being together, sex, and living life. Pam taught me to crochet, and we made crocheted bikinis and belts that we sold from the hearse.

One night as we were alone, and smoking opium, I decided it was time to do it. We were in a house on Blossom Street in Columbia when I decided to end our lives. The opium made it a dreamy, slow motion movie when I took out the knife and told her what I was going to do. She screamed, and others in the house heard it. I was restrained by some men, I don't know who, and Pam was spirited away by some women who took her into hiding. I had reached the bottom of my depression and knew I couldn't go on living. I took a massive dose of LSD, and I believe that I was trying to commit suicide.

That choice saved my life. I was alone when I did this and experienced a sense of Oneness that I had never even been close to before. I clearly saw and understood that all life was really just One life, and we were all aspects of this life and parts of God. I also saw in three dimensions before me, the circle of violence, and the cycle of pain which made me totally despondent, and cried out to God that if it was a circle, there was no end to the pain and violence, and how could I stop it.

God speaks to me in a southern accent, and said, "Just quit and get off the circle." I understood and made a promise to God. I said, "I'm done! I will never participate in violence again," and then I don't remember much else for a long time. When I woke up, or came to, or regained consciousness, I remembered my promise.

I got rid of all my weapons and became committed to Peace, both inside and outside. I managed to get word to Pam through intermediaries of my epiphany and that I was a changed man, and could I Please, Please meet with her. She agreed to the meeting in the presence of witnesses.

Somehow, I convinced her of my sincerity, and she agreed to try this thing one more time. The world had become new, and I could finally see light, and the possibility of hope that things could change. I knew lots of challenges lay ahead, and we had no money or place to live other than Talbert, but somehow everything was going to work out.

March 29, 2022

Pam and I were living in a hearse. Yep, a hearse. Talbert was a black, 1957 Cadillac hearse. It had been the vehicle in which the casket rode, and there was a little popup seat in the back where an attendant could ride. That was before Pam put it down and covered the entire back with mattresses. The inside was painted wonderful pastel colors, mostly lavender, and purple trim, with bright yellow flowered curtains that she had sewn. There was a glass divider between the driver's seat and the back, with a sliding glass window that could be closed.

The front seat for the driver and passenger was big, black, and real leather. To drive Talbert was a genuine treat. Plenty of American car V8 power, quiet, smooth, and so comfortable. Did I say 1957 Cadillac, the essence of American luxury automobile. Yes, it was a hearse, but it was a Cadillac!

After Pam taught me to crochet, I made this rack that could hold the spools of different color threads and yarns that we used to crochet the bikini's and belts and sometimes the dresses and blankets that we sold along our journeys. That rack was made to sit on the enormous dashboard in front of the passenger seat so that whoever was not driving could kick back and work while we talked and smoked weed and traveled through what was now a Max Parrish wonderland of color and adventure. There was a good bit of couch surfing with friends and sleeping in the yards and woods of welcoming people, and state parks and forests. It was just a time of letting go of everything except each other and holding tight to the moment. At that time, nothing else in the world mattered except the joy that we had with finally being together in a mad world, with no particular place to go, and no particular time to get there. Finally, I could die in the arms of my Beloved, and the rest of the world could just go away. Stoned and in Love.

I'm going to back up for a moment.

In 1964, I discovered a place that was unlike all the places I frequented in high school. I grew up playing music in rock and roll bands, beach music bands, country bands that played in those dirty roadside honky tonks where I learned to drink, and to always avoid talking to the pretty girl sitting alone at the bar. She was always bait for the big redneck boyfriend to come in and show his ass later in the evening. Which she seemed to enjoy. Always one of those in every club.

But in '64 I learned of this place. J B Gantt's, or just JB's for short. It was a seedy little greasy spoon joint located between the Town Theater and a corner gas station. It was a smallish place with a lunch counter, and just a few booths in front of the windows. You could get a real handmade burger with fries that were cut from real potatoes that they peeled right there, or a chili dog. If you were willing to risk hepatitis or food poisoning, the food was very sustaining, and carried me through a lot of my first college adventures.

But....behind the counter there was a door that led into the darkness. Before I got the courage to walk through that door, I saw a lot of unusual people going in and out, and laughing, smoking and a lot of beer was being delivered down that opening. Sometimes a loud argument and maybe a short fight could be heard coming up from down there. Out of all the clubs I had frequented, I was genuinely frightened to go through THAT door because I knew something different was going on in there.

One evening after a few beers I got the courage to follow some folks in. Ahh. It was a cellar, painted black with small tables scattered through the concrete support columns, the floor was dirty and sticky, and the air was thick with smoke. The lighting was very dim, and there were people sitting at the tables leaning in and talking of politics, poetry and heated intellectual discussions going on. In the back corner were some musicians singing songs of protest and revolution. I had found my place.

Before long, I was one of the regular musicians who gathered there to share songs that we were writing, to listen to each other, and to listen to the poets, artists, dancers, and people of all sorts that would gather there. My mind was opening up listening to the poets read their freshly written verses which slipped into my consciousness and made me see the world so differently. I began to understand that words can change the world.

It was during this time that I began to write my own songs and be willing to sing them in front of willing listeners. This was the world of the beat generation, of black turtlenecks, berets, and deep thoughts. It was near the end of the beat generation, but this was the real thing. I spent every spare minute there. This was before Pam and I first met, although sometimes I would see her there because she was working next door at the Town Theater, and came in for a quick drink, or some food.

In 1967, I did a stint of summer stock work at Hilton Head with the University of South Carolina theater program after Pam got married. When I returned, my intellectual, cellar hideaway had changed into a psychedelic wonder room. Now it was black lights, the old black concrete support columns were now painted with psychedelic scenes and made bizarre contrast to the previous decor.

Welcome in the hippie era. Magical Mystery Tour had just been released. Times were definitely changing. Music and poetry were still flowing in JB's cellar. Now there was more talk about revolution, the Chinese cultural revolution and generally the world getting worse. While Pam and I were residing in Talbert, we would frequent JB's on a regular basis and discuss our new found sense of pacifism, much to the chagrin of some of the other customers, some of whom had returned from stints with the Peace Corps, and they were more belligerent than veteran returnees.

One evening on the concrete wall outside of JB's, Dale Bailes and I were talking about things we would like to do. He expressed an idea about a place where the alternative community could get access to information and materials not commonly available, as well as a place where local artists could place their works. I had a little bit of money left from my military separation, and I said, "Why don't we do it?"

My little bit of money would get us a lawyer so that we could become incorporated and begin to sell shares to investors to get started. We found an interesting building in the Five Points area of Columbia that had been the old coal company. With a few rag tag hippie compatriots, we began the Joyful Alternative. A resource center for alternative lifestyles. Although we left the business shortly after it was up and running, it lasted for more than 30 years.

And at the end, Columbia closed the streets in Five Points for a huge gathering and the city mayor proclaimed it Joyful Alternative Day. Most of the original crew were there for a Joyful Reunion which lasted well into the wee hours of the morning, when the policemen finally told us they had to open the streets back up.

March 30, 2022

When we were building the Joyful Alternative, it was a busy, exciting, and fun time. Lots of work and idealistic hope that we were doing something that would make a difference in the world, and give people with new ways of thinking a place of community. More than just a retail store, but a safe place to come and experience new ideas, books that they might not find anywhere else, clothes that were unique, and other items for alternative lifestyles not easily found anywhere else. A place to open your mind.

I'm trying to not mention people's actual names here, but I have to say that many of us contributed to the construction and initial building of the Joyful, but it was

Barbara Howell who managed to keep the dream alive, thrive, and make it continue for more than 30 years. When it was time to close it, she talked with Pam and me, and I'm sure others as well, and cried saying she was sorry, but it was time to close it. We cried and thanked her for her lifetime of work and carrying the idea to its perfect conclusion. I found out later that Barbara died on the evening before Pam's Celebration of Life.

During the construction, Pam and I decided that we needed to stop smoking cigarettes. We were each smoking 3 packs a day. Then we found that in order to stop smoking, we would also have to stop drinking, because every time we had a drink, we wanted to smoke. And we also found that we had to stop drinking coffee, because every time we had coffee, we wanted to smoke. So, we quit smoking, alcohol, and coffee, cold turkey.

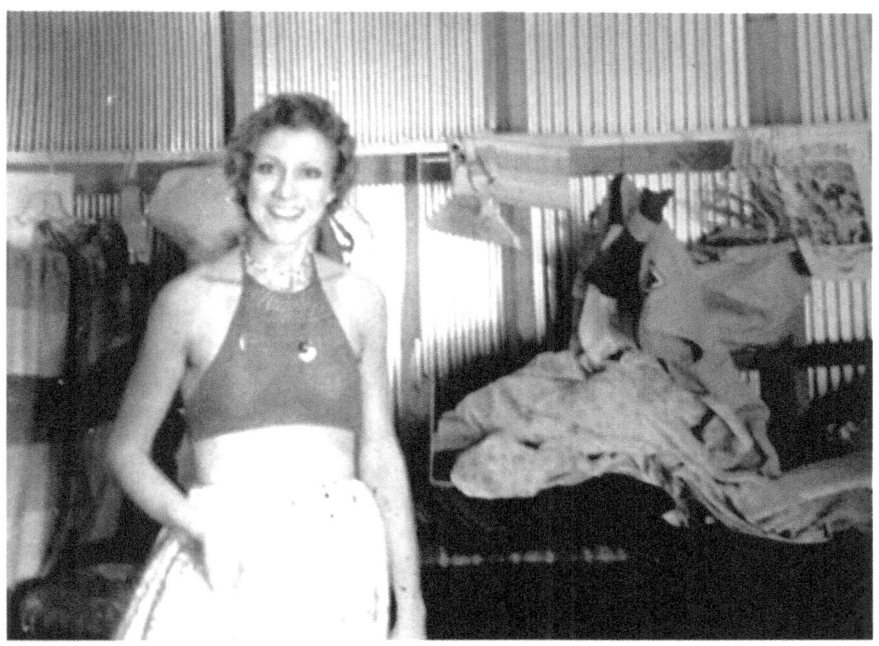

Holy crap! I don't know how we did that, with the headaches and cravings, but we supported each other and made it six weeks. At six weeks Pam said that she could not take it anymore and she was going to start smoking again. That day she found out that she was pregnant. She then said that no one would continue smoking while they were pregnant, and that was the end of cigarettes for us. Now we kept smoking pot like there was no tomorrow, but never cigarettes again.

We were still living in the hearse and had questions about whether we could possibly be parents as screwed up as we were. We actually considered abortion and made it to the abortion doctor's door with an appointment. I remember that we looked at each other, held each other, and decided that we didn't know how we could have a child because we were both crazy as dingbats living in a hearse, but we loved this new life about to come in, and knew our lives would be different now, but there would be no abortion for us.

In those days, security in Five Points was tenuous at best. There were constant break-ins and robberies at other stores in the area, so we started taking turns sleeping in the store as security. Somewhere about then, we realized that we couldn't keep doing this, and we withdrew from the Joyful working crew.

Through some friends, we had found a small house in Blythewood, which at that time was about 20 miles or so outside of Columbia. It was an old moonshiner's cabin that was pretty nasty, but the rent was cheap, and I could actually avoid rent by feeding and caring for the cattle, mending fences, and doing some general farm work.

I returned to school at the University of South Carolina and changed my major from Theater to Biology/Chemistry, thinking that I needed a real career to care for my family. Since we could get more money on the GI Bill if we were married, we decided to take that step as well. So, one day on our way to work on the cabin, we started looking for someone to legally marry us.

We figured a Justice of the Peace would be the easiest thing. Now in South Carolina at that time you could be legally married at 14, and kids came from other states just for that, but try as we might, we couldn't figure out how to find a Justice.

We remembered that we used to play music at a coffee house run by the Methodist Student Union at the University, and we thought that surely the minister there would perform the ceremony. So, we went there and knocked on the door of the minister, who opened it, and we asked if he would marry us. He said he would like to talk to us first for some counseling. We said we didn't need counseling, we just needed someone to marry us, but we had to sit and let him ask us some questions.

After a short while, we told him that we had already acquired the marriage license a month before, she was pregnant, and we wanted to get married today! He realized our situation and asked if we wanted to contact our parents or other parties to witness the event, and we said "No, it's nobody's business but ours." Then he asked if we wanted to be married in the church and we said that would be nice. Then he asked if we wanted him to dress in his robes, and we said "No, we're in overalls, and regular clothes would be fine."

So that's how we were married. George, the minister, was also the witness, and afterward we went out to work on our cabin. George didn't seem to think that we were getting married for the right reasons, and the marriage would be difficult and probably not last. We often thought about going back to see him 40 years later to show him he was wrong, but we never did.

April 4, 2022

The day we married was November 4, 1970, and began our legal relationship. After the ceremony, we got in our hearse and drove to work on our little cabin that would be our new home for the winter.

That first winter was a very cold one, and the cabin had a single, small gas heater in the back. There was a heat sucking fireplace in the front "living room," so we rarely used that room. There was a tiny kitchen/eating space, a bathroom, and a bedroom. The shower was one of those metal cubicles that gave you just enough room to be in without touching the cold sides.

We had converted the nasty little moonshiner's cabin with tobacco stains on the walls into a cozy, bright living space. We cleaned and painted everything with bright colors and homemade curtains. Pam was a master with a sewing machine and imagination. We were beginning to dream of a "back to the land" existence. Tune in, turn on, and drop out.

Because of our use of psycho active drugs, we had certainly turned on, and tuned in to our newfound reality that we were all one. Everything in the Universe is all part of the same entity. We realized that the political and economic system that we lived in was unsustainable, and the dropping out part came from a belief that if we just stopped participating in that system, it would eventually have nothing to feed on, and would eat itself.

Gosh, we were so naive, idealistic, and innocent. It was about this time that we were exposed to the book *Be Here Now*, by Richard Alpert, or Ram Dass, his newly chosen name. We resonated so heavily with the concepts presented there, because they mirrored our own experiences, but he had gone so much further.

We learned about Gurus, death of the ego, and identity with the Self instead of the self. I began to try some of the techniques in the book and found them quite comforting. We were becoming firmly rooted in a deep desire to "find God" and expand our consciousness. Yes, we did a lot of psychedelic drugs and used marijuana frequently, and we really did use them not so much recreationally, but in search of a deeper meaning in our lives.

We were way out in the country, and I had an old Chevy that I had bought right after Nam, and Pam had Talbert for transportation. I managed to get back into the university in a biology/chemistry program, thinking that would provide more opportunities for my family than a theater degree, but it meant that I was in class 6 days a week with quite a few of my classes being lab classes.

I always seemed to draw the 8 o'clock classes, and often the lab classes would keep me in town so late that I would arrive back out at the house at 10 pm or later. Then, eat with Pam, and do homework until after midnight, and leave early so that I could get a parking place and be in class by 8. This meant that I was leaving Pam alone and pregnant, out in the country by herself for a lot of the day.

One night when we were going home from a trip into Columbia, and again, very stoned, as we came into Blythewood, there in a large vacant lot was a flatbed trailer, with a large gathering of people dressed in Ku Klux Klan garb. You know, the white robes, and white pointy hats with holes for eyes, and women and children, a large bonfire, and a huge burning cross. The sight was absolutely gut wrenching, and certainly a buzz kill.

Where we had been laughing and joking on the ride home through the 20 miles of dark country roads, instantly there was fear and dread and some level of disbelief that this could be real. But it was real. It was absolutely horrifying and shook our belief of "we are all one" to the core. Blythewood was a very small community, and this gathering had more attendees than residents, so it was especially disturbing. It made our sweet little country home a good deal less comfortable. Since we and another couple were the only hippies out there, we began to wonder if we were safe. I now was very uncomfortable leaving Pam alone all day while I was at school. Then came Nona.

Nona deserves more than a chapter, and in the book that follows this, I will speak a lot more about her.

Nona was a petite, feisty young woman, recently divorced from her first husband who had spent three years in jail for refusing to be drafted. Later I would come to honor those guys who had so much commitment to their beliefs that they were willing to go to jail rather than compromise their conscious beliefs. They became kind of heroes to me. I was not that strong in those days. A lot of lives were destroyed during that time, both by the war, and by the resistance.

Nona had a small house in the woods about halfway out to our house from Columbia. She called it Mirkwood. Many wonderful parties and gatherings occurred there. We were attending one of those parties, the night after we had decided to continue the pregnancy.

Pam told Nona that she was pregnant, and I think Nona's excitement possibly eclipsed ours. We had no idea of what pregnancy meant. Pam had always thought that she would be a professional dancer and performer, and neither of us had remotely thought of ourselves as parents. I can't even say we were in shock because we were so innocent that we had zero ideas about what pregnancy meant. Nona did.

She immediately said to Pam, "Well you're going to have natural childbirth, aren't you? You're going to breast feed right?" And so many more questions. What was she talking about? You mean there is natural childbirth, and breast feeding. What?? That conversation began a lifelong relationship with this woman that taught us so much. I began to leave Pam at Mirkwood in the morning, and she would spend the day with Nona, learning to bake bread, and cook healthy, organic meals, and receive guidance into the world of motherhood in a new way.

I would pick her up at night to go home, and each day she was more radiant and excited than when I dropped her off in the morning. Nona took her to La Leche League, helped her find the right Gynecologist, and Pediatrician, and introduced us to Lamaze.

Pam took to these lessons with enthusiasm, and Nona became more than a guide, or teacher, she became a lifeline and companion for us both. There cannot be enough gratitude to her for changing our lives forever for the better. We knew we didn't want to raise children in the same way as our parents, and we just leaped into this new experience totally, and wide open to whatever it meant, and Nona was there like a light in the darkness so that we could see a way forward. Now we were hopeful again.

April 3, 2022

During that first winter, when we were home, we spent most of our time in the kitchen and bedroom, because that's all that was heated. It was cozy, but very tight. It didn't matter because it was our first home together.

Pam took to pregnancy, like everything she did. Read, talk to those who know, and get fully absorbed into the process. She weighed only about 100 pounds when she got pregnant, and her doctor told her that she needed to gain some weight for her health, and the health of the baby. Boy, we both got into that. We ate like we had never eaten before, including ice cream sandwiches and cake, and all of the newfound healthy foods that Nona was teaching her to make. Homemade bread, and biscuits, have mercy, those biscuits. Good southern biscuits are like nothing else in this world. Nona could make some biscuits, and taught Pam well. Those biscuits were still a hit in our household until her passing, although not as frequently.

We often had guests staying with us in the tiny cabin. You know, hippies always welcomed our friends in, and there was always enough room, even though often we would be sleeping in the same bed. Our daily visits to Nona's became a welcome ritual, and it seemed the gatherings there never stopped either. We really did think the old world was dying, and we were busy creating a new one.

Mother Earth News, Whole Earth Catalog, Scott and Helen Nearing, and back to the land. Mirkwood was a place like the Last Homely House, where good friends, new friends, and strangers were always welcome, and tales of faraway places, and the evils of the outside world were mixed with new ideas of how to garden organically, communes, health food stores, organic restaurants, loving behavior, and a different type of revolution.

Free Love. This term was misunderstood by many. Free Love never meant cheap love, or love that had no price. Free Love was a complete sentence with the understood subject of "You." It meant to free Love from the constraints and let Love guide the way forward. Love your neighbor did not mean screw your neighbor, or your enemy. It meant finding the Love in each that was the same part of ourselves.

Celebrate diversity. Listen to different viewpoints. Embrace the concept that we were all One, excluding nothing. It is a tough job and requires constant practice and reminding, but we felt the quickening of the world, and the awakening of the human race. This was the dawning of the Age of Aquarius. Yes indeed, we were idealistic and there were those who kept telling us we were crazy, that there would always be greed, and Love had boundaries.

But we had a vision. We could see it. We could feel it in our bodies, minds, and Spirits and were jumping off, no matter the cost. Hell, what would they do, send me to Vietnam? Already took that trip, and I could see a better way.

One night at Mirkwood, the fire had gone out, and there was no more wood. It was cold outside, and a clear full moon was shining. Nona, Pam and a friend, Jimmy, were there. Jimmy was also a Nam vet, and we took on the mission of finding firewood in the dark. We wandered around in the moonlight, stoned and almost feeling like we were on patrol, except we were laughing so hard at the strangeness that the moon shadows created in the woods.

Every time we reached down to pick up a piece of wood, it would move and transform into a snake, or some other animal and we would recoil, sometimes falling down, but laughing. Eventually, we did gather enough wood to get the fireplace and the room warm enough for us, and had a wonderful meal.

A year or so later, Jimmy would take his life, like so many of my buddies. His father also never recovered from Jimmy's suicide. We were in uncharted territory and just trying to find our way home, which no longer existed in the way that it had in our youth. Maybe *Leave it to Beaver* and *Father Knows Best* never actually did exist.

There was the afternoon when Pam and Nona and I were there alone, except for the young single mother who lived in a trailer next to Nona's house. A car with red flashing lights came driving up. Now, Mirkwood was at the end of a long dirt driveway, and if you showed up there, you were there on purpose because there was no other place out there. We kind of freaked out, thinking we were being raided by the police, since there was always pot available.

I went outside to catch them out there before they came to the door. It was actually six redneck guys looking for hippie girls to rape. By now, my hair had grown long, and I looked full on hippie. I looked in the car, and there was a handgun on the front seat, and one of the guys in the back seat was holding a large hunting knife.

Remember the promise I made to God about no more violence? God came in my head and said "How about now? Are you still willing to be nonviolent?" This was not the last time God would speak those words to me. These were tests to see if I REALLY would keep my promise. I will confess that the thoughts in my mind were wishing I had my M-16 back in my hands. I habitually reached to my side to see if it was there. If I just had it, I could resolve this situation quickly. Nope, not there, not even a pocketknife.

I began to shuck and jive the best I could, making up stuff that I had never thought of before. Every now and then, Pam would come out of the door and ask if everything was OK. Jesus, please don't do that, sweetheart. Periodically, the single mother in the trailer would be walking in front of her window, without any idea of what was going on outside, and her appearance only added to the agitation of these guys.

I talked to them for quite a while, and somehow finally convinced them that we would meet them down at the convenience store or something, I don't exactly remember, but they left, and we never saw them again, but they left a lasting impression. Sometimes, evil had a way of showing up unexpectedly, to see if your commitment to this new way of life was strong enough. It still does.

April 5, 2022

Love has a way of making timelessness real. When you are deep in Love, every moment seems to last for an eternity, and 50 years goes by and seems like a single breath. Our time in the cabin was sweet. I think I got $250 a month and spent most of the day, six days a week at the University.

I became an "A" student for the first time in my life. My prior academic experience was to get by with a barely passing grade, and sometimes not even that. It took me 16 years of schooling to discover that you were supposed to read the lesson BEFORE the class. That way you had some understanding of what the instructor was talking about, and could ask intelligent questions, and classes became more interesting.

At home, Pam was growing bigger. She gained 50 pounds for that first pregnancy and was not pleased with her new weight. She discovered that it's a lot easier putting on weight than it is to take it off. She always wanted to be thin, and she was. She told me when she looked in the mirror there was never a time when she thought she was thin enough. I think we both realized later that this was an unhealthy attitude, and in her later work with women's empowerment, it was an attitude that many, many women have.

As the pregnancy progressed, we needed to attend Lamaze birthing classes in order for me to be present in the delivery room. There were no classes locally, so every Tuesday night, we would drive to Charlotte, an hour and a half away, for class. There was no interstate highway to

Charlotte in those days, so it was all back road driving. It was exciting and gave us more time to talk...and anticipate.

My Chevy had died, and Talbert was having some mechanical issues, so we traded my car in for a used, 1970 Volkswagon super bug. It was a tight fit, but much more reliable. It's difficult to believe that with as little money as we had, that we could get a relatively new car on credit. Heck, it's not that easy now.

One night at 3 in the morning, Pam woke up in labor. We checked the frequency of the contractions, and they were only 5 minutes apart and we knew we had to go quickly, so we jumped into our car and began the 30 mile trip to the hospital.

The only hospital that would even consider allowing me in the delivery room was the brand new Lexington County Hospital, and they were quite skeptical about my participation. I was the first father at that hospital to be present in the delivery room and actually stay for the whole birth. In those days, it just was not done. I'm glad that has changed.

We barely made it to the hospital, and I suited up and went in with Pam. Birthing is such a wonderful experience. A new life coming in with all of the fluids, blood, screaming, breathing, and that unforgettable look between us as this was happening. The look of excitement, pain, and trust in her eyes at that moment made me feel more intimately connected with her than any sexual experience could ever be.

The birth, all things considered, was "easy," quick and transcendent. Laughing, crying, hugging, kissing, and touching our first son together. From the wake up to the delivery was 3 hours, including the drive.

With each of her pregnancies, Pam would begin to mind map the entire event early, and it always worked. Our first son Josh was born yelling loudly, from the moment his head popped out, and he has never hesitated to voice his opinion to this day, and he was present at the delivery of his children as well. I sincerely hope that all men will learn to be fully present and participate in the birthing experience. It is a continuation of the passion that created a new human being in the first place. Men should never be excluded from, nor be hesitant to fully experience birth.....or death. It's the same energy experience from two different viewpoints.

That morning, I was supposed to take an important organic chemistry exam. The professor had said that he would not give a makeup exam to anyone for any circumstances except an act of God. That class was one of those large classes with probably more than a hundred students in the lecture hall. When I raised my hand and explained that I would need to take a makeup exam, he said no. I told him that I was in the delivery room for the birth of my child, and I considered that an act of God.

He was dismissive and said that the delivery room was no place for a man, and that my place was to be at that exam. My excitement from the birth switched to that anger that I was carrying, and I walked down to the front of the lecture hall in front of all the other students and began to use some pretty vulgar and threatening language explaining to him that birthing WAS an act of God, and I guess I became physically threatening, so I was removed from the class.

I never took the exam, and that's the only class where I ever received a failing grade. Even with my newfound

Oneness experience, I could see I still had triggers, and the anger had not gone away, it was just sleeping deep inside, snuggled up next to the guilt and shame I was repressing.

The rest of the summer passed quickly, and I could see that sometimes Pam was struggling with sleep deprivation, and constant attention that was necessary to care for a newborn. I did the best I could.

We developed a method where, when he would wake to nurse during the night, I would change the diaper while Pam nursed him. That way we could get him back to sleep, and neither of us would have to stay awake long, but it was still tough on her. During the whole Vietnam experience, I never actually slept. I was always awake on some level, and I used to laugh at people who would complain of lack of sleep. I developed a whole new respect for nursing mothers, which has never left me.

At the end of the summer semester, I signed up for an elective class where we could propose a project of any kind, and do unsupervised work, and return at the end to report on how it had gone. I chose to go to the woods and practice yoga and meditation, and my project was accepted.

Pam and I were losing our little cabin, so with a tent and screen room, we moved into our Volkswagen and off to stay in the woods. We would camp in the national forest and do our practice of yoga and as much meditation as we could with a newborn, but we certainly communed deeply with the forest. The park service would only allow us to stay in the same place for two weeks, so we would just move to another part of the forest and stay two more weeks and so forth.

Fall in the North Carolina mountains is beautiful, especially when you are living so close to the Earth. Campfires, cooking on the open fire, washing dishes in the stream, and just being with each other and our child. It was Heaven on Earth. As the weather became colder, we decided to come down and find a more permanent place to live.

We had some friends in Charlotte that we shared a house with for a while, and several other places, but eventually we needed to get a place of our own. Nona came through and found us a small house in a nice area of Columbia, about 4 miles from the University, and biking distance. The Shandon area of Columbia was quiet, with wide streets, and very little traffic. It made biking so easy that we rarely had to start the car.

We both had bikes with baby seats on the back where Josh could ride. In those days, there were no helmets or safety gear, and we rode everywhere with Josh on the back, or in a backpack. I got an A in the class for my experiences, and life was good. During this time, we acquired our 1965 Volkswagen micro bus, which soon would become our next home.

April 7, 2022

Another morning. It's dark. I wake up now at 3 am, or 4 am to another morning, or is that mourning? Telling our story seems important somehow, although I still don't know why. In the years when Pam and I were trying to write a book about our lives, she kept asking me, "Why would anyone want to hear about our lives? Everybody has a story of their life." I don't know, but I think it means something.

We are not our story, we are much more, and everyone does have a story. I realize that I am skipping huge chunks of detail and interesting pieces in order to keep this small enough for Facebook. Ah, Facebook.

I woke up yesterday and got ready to write and found that Pam's account had been locked. I don't know why, perhaps because I have been downloading the enormous number of Porch Of Peace broadcasts that she did. But anyway, I was locked out until I went through a lengthy process to get back in. Your encouraging and enlightening comments help me keep doing this.

The next house was on Ott Road, and our time there was wonderful. Pam began to be interested in plants, and I would bring her cuttings or unusual plants from the University greenhouse. She filled the sun porch with all kinds of flowering plants. There was even a sweet potato that she put in a vase of water, that grew such long vines, that they wrapped around the ceiling of the porch.

It was a safe neighborhood. We could walk or bike for miles with friendly neighbors who had lovely floral landscaping with azaleas, camellias, tulips, dogwoods, and so many different flowers. Columbia is a beautiful place in the late winter and early spring. Josh was growing and had his first birthday at that house.

Our closest neighbors, whose tiny house was just a few feet from our bedroom window, were Kat and Swede. A biker couple who seemed very out of place in the neighborhood. Kat was Rubenesque with a sweet face, and Swede was big, tall and intimidating wearing his gang colors and his panhead Harley Davidson motorcycle. They had their issues, just like we all do, but they turned out to be wonderful friends.

There was a day when I was working outside in the front yard, and a carload of fraternity type guys stopped and started harassing me, I guess because of the long hair, and again God came in and said "How about now? Still nonviolent?" Just as things were getting out of hand, Swede came rumbling up on his bike, walked over and asked, "Donald T, are these guys bothering you?" There was no need for violence. Swede with his long red hair and beard was so intimidating that they very quickly jumped back in their car and quietly sped away. You just can't judge someone by their looks. He was actually a sweet and loving guy. As long as you didn't piss him off.

I was having some stomach pain issues, and I went to my old family doctor, and discovered that I was developing an ulcer. I tended to worry a lot, and my deeper issues were still cooking in there. I was in a period where I thought that if I just denied being a veteran, and forgot about my experiences, they would eventually go away. It doesn't work like that.

Anyway, miraculously, instead of giving me medication, he suggested that I try meditation. As it happened, there was a Transcendental Meditation class being offered near the University at a special rate for students, so I signed up. It was a life-changing experience. It's a process of quieting the mind. Turning off the mental chatter, and "transcending" into a place of no thought. No thought at all. A quiet place of awareness, peace, and rest.

There was one day in the training when I was running late for class, and couldn't get there on my bike, so Swede put me on the Harley and took me to meditation class. Man, that was a fun ride. I also recognized that place of "Get the f*** out of the way everybody, I've got to get to my meditation!!" I was learning that the meditation started long before the class. It was helping me a lot.

During this time, the owners of the house called and offered to sell us the house for $5,000 dollars. No matter how hard we tried to get the money from the bank, or help from relatives, we could not come up with $5,000 dollars. Not having access to money became a running theme for us.

When I graduated in August of 1972, Pam and I decided to take a road trip in the micro bus. We left on a month-long camping trip that took us all the way to northern Vermont and back, through the mountains. A slow ride using back roads all the way. We left with $100, for a month-long trip, and came back with change. Gas was often 15 cents a gallon.

On the way back home, we stopped to see Nona in Durham, NC. She had opened a great little restaurant called the Blue Bird Cafe. I was looking in the paper and saw an advertisement for a job at a drug company in Research Triangle Park, and decided to apply. They were impressed with my skills and offered me a great starting position, but we would have to move to Durham, and start right away.

The salary looked fantastic, and the opportunity for growth and more education was appealing.

We left our house in Columbia and just moved to Durham. We didn't have a house yet, so Nona let us stay in the back of the Cafe, and Pam became the "Omelet Lady," while I started work in a huge corporation while sleeping in the back of the restaurant.

Our friend Steven R. Miller was a student at Duke and offered us the opportunity to move in with him and his housemate. We didn't think it was a good idea to share a house with a couple of college guys when we had a 1 year old child, but they assured us it would be alright, and they baby proofed the house and we moved in. Two college guys, me and Pam, and Josh. They were wonderful. Pam would cook for us like a family, conversation was always lively, and I went to work each day. In a very short time, my new salary had paid off all our school debts, and things seemed to be working out. Then I began to realize what I had signed up for. No amount of meditation was going to make this okay.

April 8, 2022

Parts of this post will have some information that is somewhat graphic and some of you may not want to read parts of this.

When I accepted the job at the drug research company, it seemed like the dream job. Great salary, fabulous benefits package, opportunities to continue with my education, and all the other things that one could want in a career. I was the only assistant to this wonderful Asian man who, at that time, was one of the only people in the world who had developed a method for monitoring the nerve impulses at the synaptic cleft. Which means we could take a tiny nerve impulse, capture it, amplify it, run it through an oscilloscope, and get a picture of the signal.

We could do this real time. It meant we could take living tissue, get a base line of the nerve signal, and then administer drugs to the tissue and see what in the chain of events of the movement of the signal was being affected by the drug. We were working specifically with new drugs for surgical anesthesia. It was fascinating work.

Pretty much anything we wanted could be ordered just by calling up the supply person and telling them what we wanted. We had access to the latest information on our interests just by calling up the company library, which was connected to an early form of what would become the internet, and within a half hour we could have even newly published research papers delivered to our office on a little cart. In 1972 this was difficult for me to believe.

During the initial interview they had asked if I was okay with vivisection work. I knew that I had dissected frogs in my lab classes and felt I could handle that. I really didn't understand what that word meant. Each day did start with the killing and dissection of a frog, to get a nerve fiber and connecting tissue removed and placed in a special container, so that we could keep the tissue from dying, so we could monitor the nerve signal when stimulated.

After a while, we switched to laboratory rats. This began to be uncomfortable to me, and I expressed my feelings to my supervisor, but I managed to keep going for a while. Then, at the end of each day, I would take my rat carcass down to the basement to be placed with all the other carcasses being fed into a furnace. There were a lot. That's when I realized that they were testing on all kinds of animals. I'm not going any further with this description.

Let's just say that I was having a breakdown. My supervisor, who was a wonderful and sensitive man said that with my beliefs, he was surprised I could do this work. I said that I couldn't, and asked to leave. I was sent to the HR department who said they realized that they had placed me in a job that was not what I had originally applied for, and they offered me quite a few positions in different departments. I refused all of them.

At the end of the process, the person guiding me through this interview told me that if I quit this job, I would not be able to get another job in this field because they would give me a bad review, and they were concerned that I would take the knowledge that I had gained there to another company. I just wanted OUT and I didn't think they could blackball me from any other job. They could, and did. After I left there, I applied for many, many jobs and they all declined me because of references from the drug company.

I went from making lots of money, to no money, no job, no prospects. It was winter and the Watergate investigation was well under way. To make a very long story shorter, I finally got a job on a survey crew as a rod man, the lowest position on a survey crew, making $2.30 an hour with no benefits.

That winter was cold, and I spent my days cutting brush and trees to clear the view for the person sighting the lines for the surveys. To demonstrate how difficult employment was then, the crew chief of our 3 man crew had a doctorate from Duke University, the instrument man had a master's degree from the University of North Carolina, and me with my bachelor's degree from the University of South Carolina, and our combined salaries was less than I had made at the drug company.

There is so much more I could say about the pharmaceutical business, but I may have already said too much.

In the spring we found a little cabin outside of Durham that was small and pretty funky, but it was in the country at the end of a little tractor path and seemed quiet. It had no inside toilet, but the outhouse was out back, and it turns out it was in a huge field of daffodils. Morning poops were kind of cold, but looking at the most beautiful art piece you can imagine.

We had many visitors there and some parties. At one of these parties, a biker friend of ours met a guy who was making clinical grade LSD at Duke University. A business transaction occurred, and they told us they wanted to pay us a finder's fee for introducing them. We declined because we never wanted to be in the drug business, we just like to do drugs.

They said they felt they needed to do something, so they asked if they could give us some of the LSD. We said "Sure," thinking we would get some to take. They gave us 750 doses in a bag and said thank you. We sat there at the table after they left. We were stunned. Then we looked at each other across the table and said, "I wonder how long it would take to eat 750 hits of acid? Let's find out." And that decision sent us into the wild and wonderful next chapter in our lives and changed us forever.

April 9, 2022

The little cabin we were living in during those days we called Winkler's. The man who rented it to us was an old farmer, who lived about a half mile up the tractor path and seemed harmless enough. His invalid mother lived with him.

The cabin was small, and had a screen porch, a small kitchen, and the ceilings were only about six and a half feet tall. Some of my taller friends had to stoop to get around in some areas. I remember that one window in the front room had no glass, it had plastic over the empty space. I was going to fix that if we stayed long enough. But it was warm, and private, and quiet most of the time.

Mr. Winkler offered me space to garden if I wanted, and so I planted my first organic garden in a patch behind the barn. I would help him plow and mow sometimes. This was my first experience with tractors, but I took to it easily, and it was meditative work once you learned how to operate the machine. I was still working on a survey crew, and each morning I drove the company 4 wheel drive Blazer to pick up the other two crew members to start the work day. Most days I carried my guitar and practiced during a lunch break. Pam and I played and sang a lot at the cabin as well.

As spring moved further towards summer, Mr. Winkler asked if we had seen the Jack Um Lanterns. I asked if he was talking about lightning bugs, or fireflies. He said, "No, but they are like lightning bugs, but bigger and more orange." We would often sit on the screen porch at night and sometimes go out for evening walks down the path, or in the fields behind the cabin. Then one night we did see them...the Jack Um Lanterns.

They were bright orange/white globes that floated in the hollers down by the creek and up into the woods, and they were a good bit larger than fireflies, which were also present in large numbers. It was a little bit unnerving to see these things, and kind of gave me goose bumps. They stayed far enough away so that I never was able to discover what they really were, and in a way, I didn't want to.

One night around Pam's birthday, July 6, we had some friends visiting from Columbia, and sleeping on the porch. It was late in the evening, and we were quieting down for the night when I heard horses coming down the path to our house. It was dark, with no moon, and I was straining to see who would be coming down at this time of night. The others on the porch heard them as well.

As the sounds of the horse's hooves and whinnying came closer, I kept trying to see them. Then they were really close, and passing by just in front of the cabin. We all looked and listened intently. They passed right by, but there were no horses. We could hear them clearly, but they weren't there. They passed on by, and we were all spooked and didn't know what to do.

There was little sleep that night, but there were plenty of Jack Um Lanterns, more than usual. The next morning, close examination of the yard, and path revealed absolutely no trace of horse tracks. Most everyone left that day, and our quiet life began to unravel. We told Mr. Winkler about hearing horses in the night. He told us that the cabin had been a stage stop in the 1800's and that there had been a massacre there, and odd things happened often. It was also about that time that Mr. Winkler changed.

He started drinking heavily, and appearing at the cabin during the day when Pam was there alone with our son. He would guzzle down a lot of whiskey at his house, and then walk down the tractor path to our cabin, and want to talk with Pam.

When she told me, I confronted him, and he said he wanted us to help him care for his mother if we were going to be living in the cabin for such cheap rent. I told him we were not interested in doing that, and that we would be leaving soon, and he was not under any circumstances to visit Pam while I was away. He still did, so Pam started leaving during the day. This is when Nona again enters the story.

Nona and a couple of other young women had rented one of the old farmhouses in a place called Cedar Grove, about 20 miles outside of Hillsborough as part of an unintentional community of renegade refugees from Chapel Hill, and Durham. Pam would visit with Nona and the girls in the day while I was at work. This was our introduction to our first real spiritual family, the Cedar Grove, Hurdle Mills ONEderful family.

I would go there after work instead of home and have some time of rest and spiritual renewal with the companionship of Nona and our newfound community. I took my first hit of the 750 doses of LSD, and walked out into the early evening mist in the pastures, took off my clothes and discovered the beauty of the world. I listened to the sounds of the ending of the day, heard the cows talking their cow language, which I understood, and they came close and warmed me with their breath and bodies. The mist rose up from the fields and tenderly caressed me like my mother used to do. I re-membered my place in the universe, and just wanted this to continue.

We knew we had found our family of choice. Once the story of our living situation became known, we were immediately offered a place at Brown Earth, which we graciously accepted, and some of our new community helped us pack our stuff and move to our new home, and we bid farewell to Winkler's and left behind all the weirdness of that place except for the memories.

I quit my job with the surveying company, and started driving a tractor for the local dairy, and gardening with Kenny Bob, the other resident of Brown Earth, and the generous man who invited us in to live there. We developed a deep and extremely close relationship with Kenny Bob, which continues to this day, even though we rarely see one another.

We received a small salary, and we each also got a gallon of fresh raw milk every day. There were always plenty of people at the table, and plenty of music and singing during the evenings. The LSD helped with community, and others brought in various forms of psychoactive drugs. Each day started with a dose of LSD, and there was a large salad bowl of what we called mescaline on the kitchen table, and whenever the "sparkle" of the day would wain, we would just stick our finger in the bowl, scoop up some and sparkle on. Most of the time we didn't even bother to put on clothes. Naked gardening is truly wonderful. There was always music, and an intense sense of close brother/sisterhood.

Brown Earth was the center for the community cooperative buying club. We had several refrigerators and freezers, and the big truck would deliver the bulk goods, and we would break them down into the different parcel sizes that the other members of the community had ordered, and people would just drop by and pick up their goods.

It meant we were always visiting with people and sharing our vision of the new world we were creating where Love, sharing and cooperation would be the norm. There were lots of bonfires, potluck meals, and music, music, music. I was writing songs again, and hearing music that needed to be written. People can you feel it? Love is in the air. People can you feel it? Love is everywhere.

One day we had a community coop meeting along with an afternoon potluck meal. Someone put LSD in the punch, so to speak. I DO NOT recommend nor condone this action. I don't know who did it, but it was the best 3 day coop meeting in history. Many lives were changed during that meeting. Consciousness was definitely expanding.

April 12, 2022

1973 This was our Summer of Love. Brown Earth was such a magical place. Our gardens were bountiful. We had so much produce, that we were selling to the local farmer's market, and they came and picked the produce up and left us money. The co-op truck brought us wonderful food, and we were able to just garden, play music, have gatherings pretty much every night with bonfires, dance in the moonlight, sing old songs and new songs, and just Love one another.

We rarely had to go into town. We had several dogs, and a goat that thought she was a dog. Whenever a car would arrive on the long driveway, the dogs would run out to greet it, and the goat would run along with the dogs, I'm sure she knew she was one of the pack.

It seemed like that summer lasted a long time, but fall would inevitably arrive with the brisk winds and changes in the air. The Earth was moving again. All the acid was gone, and there were no withdrawals, it just ended. So, to answer an earlier question, it took about 3 or 4 months to eat 750 hits of acid...with the help of our friends.

Our time at Brown Earth ended with the changing of the seasons, and we left in our micro bus for Columbia. Again, we had no place to live yet, so we set up housekeeping in the bus and moved from place to place. We knew quite a few people with land who never seemed to mind if we were camping there.

As the weather grew colder, we knew we would have to move inside. My parents had purchased a mobile home as a temporary living situation while they were transitioning from the funeral home to a more permanent place. The mobile home was on a nice plot of land with pine trees and azaleas, and they asked if we would like to stay there. It was empty then, and they were concerned that it would be vandalized if it stayed empty for very long.

We moved into the mobile home, and I once again managed to get into the university in a recording and video program. We also started playing a regular gig at the Forum Lounge each weekend with Pam's brother as a trio. The Forum was a unique place. It was always packed on the nights we were playing, and was a club atmosphere with lots of smoke, drink, and conversation. The owner really loved us, and our music, and bent over backwards to keep us playing.

Pam was known as the woman who would nurse her child on stage, and he said she couldn't do that in the Forum. She told him that he could take care of Josh while we sang then. He relented, and it was an interesting thing. She could be nursing Josh discreetly while belting out a blues song. Have mercy, that woman could sing, and multi-task.

Often the crowd would include businesspeople wearing suits, bikers in their colors, and over at one table were the people from the ashram who would sit in meditation and order nothing but water, and Wally, the owner would allow it because of the music.

We began to notice that when we were playing, some people would be crying. We wondered if it was certain songs, or notes that would trigger these responses from people and I began trying to understand what would cause such intense emotional responses from the audience. I never figured it out. Each time we would play, we asked God to sing us, and then try to get out of the way, and let the music do whatever it was going to do.

If we were successful in getting out of the way, the music worked. If we were performing and trying to make it happen, it was just a show, and was less effective. We began to trust in the power of music, and right up through our last concert, the week before she died, that's how we approached playing music.

It was also about this time that we learned that we would be blessed with a second child. I'm glad we had the comfort of the mobile home, and the "security" of a steady weekend music gig to carry us through this one.

Pam's labor with Jesse was extremely short. In fact she was saying she was having to hold him in while getting to the hospital. The good old Lexington County Hospital remembered us, and the birth was lightning fast. I barely had time to park the bus and get to the delivery room before he was born.

We played every Saturday night from 9 to 1 during the pregnancy, and Jesse was born on a Saturday night at about 9, and we were back playing the following Saturday, with a newborn. Life gets much busier with two children.

Playing in the club atmosphere also had some drawbacks. There was always a lot of smoke, and even though we had quit smoking years before, 4 hours of singing in the club left us feeling like we had smoked a pack of cigarettes. It was like doing a heavy workout while smoking.

Pam began to develop some sinus issues from the smoke, and, we were eating a lot of milk, and other dairy products. At some point, she became addicted to nose spray to keep her sinuses open. After a while, if she didn't use the nose spray, she couldn't breathe through her nose.

On day she came across Arnold Ehret's book about a mucusless diet. She was convinced that this would help, so we stopped dairy and began to modify our diet. It helped some, but we needed bigger changes.

As the changes from the dairy free diet began to show improvements in health, she also discovered Viktoras Kulvinskas's *Survival into the 21st Century*, and the Hippocrates Health Institute, and began to explore a raw foods diet. Mostly home-grown sprouts of various kinds, and fruits and vegetables. We were now vegetarians, but not quite only raw foods.

We moved to McClellanville, SC with the help of some really good friends there and ended up in a "free" house just off Highway 17. McClellanville was a small shrimping village halfway between Charleston and Georgetown, SC. We were walking distance from the marsh which opened up to Bull's Island refuge and wildlife area.

It was a drive, but the beach at Sullivan's Island wasn't far away, and we started to go there every morning, and Pam would pack her face with sea mud, and bathe in the salt water while the children and I would play in the ocean, body surf, and explore the tidal pools, and sand dunes. Gradually, her sinuses cleared, and we all became nice and tanned and much healthier.

Sometimes we would play a gig, sometimes I would work as a carpenter. Sometimes I worked on a sailboat down in Georgetown, but one way or another we were making it work. We went back to Columbia to play one last gig at the Forum as it was closing. We played for opening night, and every Saturday for 2 years, and we played the last set as it closed. When the Forum closed, it was the end of an era.

Winter was beginning to approach, and it looked like the widening of Highway 17 was going to take our house in McClellanville, so we needed to move again. We found a small farmhouse outside of Blythewood that a friend was leaving, so we moved there. It was even farther out of town than our other houses. It was quite remote. I think this was 1976.

We got word that Butterworth's health had gotten bad, and we thought it would be helpful if she left New York and came to live with us for a while and maybe we could take care of her and help her recover. It seems her kidneys and liver were failing. She was now in her late 70's, and the years of vodka and cigarettes were beginning to take their toll. I drove to New York and picked her up, along with her two cats, and brought her home with us. We had no idea what a wild winter that would turn out to be.

Donald T. McMahon

April 13, 2022

Before I go any further with the story of winter with Butterworth, there are some other parts that I need to speak to.

I started telling our story on Facebook because when Pam transitioned, someone asked me to tell about how we met, and someone else asked me to explain how we could have such a wonderful relationship after 50+ years, that they wanted a relationship like ours. They thought it was perfect.

Whenever people asked this when Pam was alive, she would always say to them, "You're only seeing us now, you don't know all the work that went into our relationship. It wasn't always like this. Long term relationships take a lot of work and a lot of compromise, and not giving up."

If anyone gets anything from these stories, I hope that it's this lesson. If you want the perfect relationship, don't settle for anything less. And also, that everything is in perfect order all the time. When it looks awful or weird, it's only because we can't see the whole story of life.

Our lives and story are a demonstration of what Love can do. Every time we were in desperate trouble and could not see any way to resolve whatever situation we were in, and we had tried everything we knew, and just gave up, the answer would always come from what we came to call "The Unknown Quarter," or Spirit, or God, or whatever you choose to call the creator of all that is.

Pam used to say, "If you can't trust God in the dark, you should find another God." This is a lesson we learned over and over and over. Authenticity and integrity. Only be who you are, and always make the choice that you know in your heart is correct, even when no one is looking. Even though we chose a life of experimenting with new ways of living, and of child rearing, and of relationship with the world, we rarely lost sight of these principles, and we were always seeking expanded consciousness and a deeper connection with Spirit.

For all practical purposes, our marriage was actually very conventional. We chose monogamy because we felt that we did not have the capacity to have sexual relations with others while having a sexual relationship with each other. Others in our communities were having multiple partners, and seemed to be able to do that, but we knew we couldn't. We Loved each other so completely and fully, there was just no room for other sexual partners, so neither of us ever had a sexual affair after we were married.

That doesn't mean that we couldn't Love other people, it was just that physical sex was a line that would never be passed. Love is much bigger than sex, although sexual union was a huge part of our relationship.

We also decided that we had to have a division of labor in the marriage, and it had nothing to do with male/female roles. There needed to be a "home maker" if there was going to be a home, and that was usually Pam. I was chosen to play the role of provider mostly because with my college degree, it was assumed I could make more money. Boy, that was a joke. During the last years of her life, I would apologize frequently for not being a better provider.

I never seemed to be able to find a way to create much financial security. Pam would always tell me gently that she was so happy, that all of our dreams had come true. She said that she never wanted a lot of money, and that we always had just enough.

We had a comfortable home, even though it's a funky hippie house, our children all made it to adulthood, we owned our home and cars, and had no debt at 65. I was never able to create enough money for life insurance, or retirement or anything like that. We always figured we would "bop till we dropped" She did exactly that. She laughed and danced and sang until the split second that she left. You go girl!!!

Wherever we were, our home was always open to strangers and friends alike and somehow, we always had enough food to share and space to rest. Even when it was just a campsite.

I think it was when we were living in the mobile home and playing at the Forum, that we began to play in prisons. Some would call it a prison ministry, but we didn't think of it that way. We were just carrying the music to those in need, and we also had quite a few friends in prison by then.

In those days, it was difficult to get into prisons to play. We had to be affiliated with some religious group to get in, so we just did whatever to make it work. We have never been joiners of any particular kind of religion and have been perfectly happy working within Christian, Muslim, Hindu, Jewish, Pagans, Native People or any religious group, we just never became members.

We found that all groups have fundamental ideas of Love, Compassion, Sharing, some form of "Do Unto Others as you would have them Do Unto You," and a belief in a greater Consciousness. That was all fine with us, and our congregation, or fellowship was anyone that we met on our journey.

Pam always gave money to the homeless or jobless, and there were never restrictions on the money. If they needed to buy drugs there was no scolding or reprimanding. Her thing was always, "What Can Love Do Here?" When we would find ourselves in strange and unusual situations she would frequently turn and look at me and say, "What Can Love Do Here?"

There was also a time when we got really upset about something that was going on along our property line, and Pam couldn't get close to the property line without high blood pressure and feeling like she was going to have a heart attack. We had a friend come through from New Zealand who was an Avatar Master, and he could see her dilemma and asked if she would be open to a way to fix the stress.

Of course, she agreed and he said that every time she ran into some situation that caused her stress she should just step back, take a breath and say, "What an interesting creation." It's amazing, but that became a fixture in our lives and often, when things looked really bad, we would just stop, look and each other and say, "What an interesting creation," and more often than not, we would begin to laugh and whatever was causing the tension would become nothing more than a moment of confusion.

I can see there is much more I need to say about these things before I go on with the story, but I will have to continue later, as the chores of the day have made themselves known. I will be back in touch as soon as I can.

April 15, 2022

I want to continue this morning with a couple more stories about our time singing and working in prisons. Somewhere around 1974, we were only able to carry music into prisons if we were affiliated with some accepted religious group. We never believed in proselytizing, or in trying to convert anybody to anything or religious belief, we just felt that the music would lift people's spirits up, and just for a moment give them some relief, comfort, and a little peace. We figured God could take care of the rest.

One particular night around Valentine's Day, we were playing for a minimum-security prison, and the religious group that was supposed to escort us in were late. Prison regulations are very strict, and when they schedule you for an hour and a half, that's all you get, and if you're late, that's less time you have with the inmates.

Since we were late, and the inmates were already restless, we decided to just play as much music as we could in the hour that we had left. We started playing and didn't stop until the time was up. This didn't give the religious group any time to speak about their particular brand of religion. By the end, the inmates were super happy, and excited.

Since this was a minimum-security facility, we had brought our 3 year old son Josh in with us, and Pam was quite pregnant with Jesse, our second son. At the end of the concert, many inmates were crying, and Josh, who had a big stash of valentines asked if he could give valentines to the inmates. It was a little scary, but we said yes he could, and the guards allowed it. Josh went all through the rows of inmates giving each one a little valentine. It was touching to watch.

There was one very large black man in the back who appeared very sad, with a scowl on his face. He was the kind of guy that you crossed the street if you saw him coming in your direction. When Josh got to him, this man said, "I bet you don't have one for me." Josh looked right up at this man and said, "I have one more," and reached up to hand it to him. The man burst into tears, started sobbing, and picked Josh up and hugged him so close. All of our children were tow heads, so the contrast of the tiny white-headed child in the arms of this big, scary black man was a transcendent image that has stayed with me my entire life.

This was my child, and I didn't know this man, but it felt like it was okay. There was not a dry eye in the entire auditorium, including the guards. I thought to myself that this is the genuine work that we are on earth to do. This is the example that every religion taught. Pure Love can lift any and everyone. I would like to think that some long-lasting healing came from that interaction, but I'll never really know because I never saw any of those men again in my life. It was just a moment, then we were ushered out.

The next story is a little different because it took place in a women's maximum-security facility. Women's prison is very different than male prison. The vibes are even more intense. When we went to this particular prison, obviously we couldn't carry Josh in, but Pam was VERY pregnant. I think she was probably in the last six weeks, so her belly was large like a basketball.

When we went in, the audience was already seated, and it was stark. On the left side were all white women, and on the right side were all black women, kind of like the bride's side and the groom's side at a wedding. There was no crossing, or mingling.

At the front of each side, up near the stage, there was a special comfortable chair in front of all the rest, kind of like a throne. On the black side there was a rather formidable looking black woman seated on the "throne," with a white woman like a servant at her side, and on the white side was the reverse. A formidable looking white woman was seated on the "throne," with a black "servant" at her side.

There was not a smile anywhere in this group. It was grim. This was one of those times when Pam would whisper to me, "What can Love do here?" and I didn't have a clue. We began to play and there was no response. No clapping, no smiling, no tears, no expression at all. Just blank stares as if we weren't even there. After a few songs, and no response, as a man, I felt like I needed to cross my legs, because these women would castrate me if they could.

So Pam began to sing "I'm a woman," which is a blues song about the power of a woman in all things, and she was belting this song out with authority, and as pregnant as you can get. At the end of that song there was thunderous applause from both sides of the isle, with much screaming, and the black woman got up from her "throne" and had her "servant" bring the "throne" up on the stage. She looked at Pam so deeply and said, "Mama, I believe you need this chair."

Most of the time in prisons, the guards would not allow us to touch the inmates, but this woman hugged Pam with a tenderness and Love for a while, and no guard intervened. The whole audience applauded and yelled out something like, "Yes woman!!!" They tolerated me, which made me feel blessed.

For the rest of the concert, they were fully present and engaged. The concert was fantastic, and we were all uplifted. For me, this was right at the top of all the concerts we ever played. When the time was up, and the guards came in to usher us out, the women began to chant and refuse to leave. All of a sudden, in the blink of an eye, things got very tense.

The women were refusing to leave, and the guards were getting more agitated. The black "queen" spoke to one of the guards closest to us and said that if they would allow us to play one more song, they would go peacefully back to their cells. In all the other prison experiences that we had, that would have been an ugly end, with the guards forcibly removing everyone, but in this case, they looked around and agreed.

There was a lot of yelling, and cheering, but soon they were all seated again. I think this is when we began using the song "You know who your friends are by looking in their eyes" as our closing song, which we used to close every concert from then until our last concert. After we ended the song, there was much crying, but they quietly got up and filed out, with many Thank You's. We never saw or heard from any of these women again.

The experience of our music had taken an unexpected turn, and the full weight of responsibility of carrying such a powerful tool began to show itself to us. It did, and still does make me humble, and somewhat intimidated every time I play. I still experience stage fright before every performance.

As long as Pam and I would get out of the way, and let the music do its work, it always worked. This gift and talent was never taken lightly, and we were always thankful and respectful of the power of the music. Thanks for listening, and with the next episode I'll get back to the Butterworth

Winter. I Love you all and am so blessed that you have the interest about our shenanigans.

April 16, 2022

It's this morning at 4:16 AM on 04/16/2022. I don't know the significance of these numbers, but I've been noticing strange number patterns lately. I know I took a slight diversion with the prison stories, but I'm just following this journey telling wherever my heart leads me.

I've been advised by several people that if I intend for our story to be a book, that I should stop writing it on Facebook. I'm not sure how I feel about that. Somehow, I think Pam wants me to tell this freely on her page with respect for her feelings and honor all of the people who have followed her and supported her on this platform.

I am in awe of the magnitude of power that her Porch Of Peace Live Broadcasts have made as I have heard from so many people from all over the world. I have been overwhelmed by the beauty and impact that she has made in people's lives, and the world that I have been blessed to witness both before and since her passing.

I don't know what the long-range plan is for this, but for now I'm going to continue with respect as I am guided by my heart, and whatever this is that I'm hearing in my head from Pam. We were never concerned with commercial success anyway, and maybe that's why we never achieved financial success in that way. We have always just shared Love and Music without reservation, wherever and whenever we could and if that's our legacy, then I'm good with that.

Now, Butterworth Winter.

By the fall when I drove to New York and gathered Betty, her cats, and her belongings and delivered her to our little house in Blythewood, I think she was in her 70's and was suffering from a lifetime of alcohol and nicotine abuse, as well as a pretty tough life all around.

She and her sister were children of a family that ran a famous and successful publishing business in London. From her stories, they were left unsupervised a lot, and frequently got up and had breakfast of leftover cake and champagne from her parents' parties. She spent a lot of time with the rich and famous of London and Paris and had great stories of Dylan Thomas and Django Reinhardt, and others.

She survived the London bombings of World War II, and her husband was a British pilot who was killed early in the war. She told me vivid stories of those times which always kept me on the edge of my seat. She lived with the Bedouins for a while. There is so much to tell of her life, that you will have to wait for the book for any more of that.

When she arrived in Blythewood, it was not what she expected.

She thought that we had some kind of successful farmstead like she was accustomed to in England, and we were just poor hippies living in an old house in the woods with 2 children and lots of visitors. There was an adjustment period, and she was in very bad physical health with failing kidneys and liver. She continued to smoke continuously, and drink heavily.

Pam and I had moved further into a raw food diet, and she made gallons of fresh sprouts. Not just alfalfa sprouts, but bean sprouts and several other kinds of sprouts as well. She made them by soaking the seeds in gallon jars, pouring off the liquid and rinsing daily. Butterworth was absolutely horrified by our diet, as she preferred mostly meat, and nearly raw. She watched Pam make the sprouts and told her that she didn't want the sprouts, but she was interested in the rinse water, so she would take the first soaking water and leave it for some days until it fermented. Then she strained it, and that's what she drank. A lot of it.

It was a very cold winter that year, and the house was not well insulated. We had a single LP gas heater, and a fireplace. If I can give any advice here, it's never to use a fireplace for heat. I think you would do better to cover the fireplace and put a candle in front of it.

There were many interesting visitors because we knew quite a few people who were drug smugglers and dealers, but they had great stories and Butterworth was very interested in their stories and listened for hours as they would tell her of their exploits in South America, Jamaica and generally about the "business." She loved it.

Pam could out smoke any of these guys and frequently would have them crawling out of the house, begging her to stop shotgunning reefer smoke in their faces. She would always tell them, "When the roll of the hard core is called, are you with me, or are you just pussies?" Where marijuana would put me to sleep, it seemed to energize her.

It was a wild, cold winter. By spring, Butterworth's kidneys and liver were functioning well, she was tanned from sitting outside, and her attitude had improved dramatically, but she was ready to get back to New York and civilization. This time a close friend drove her back to New York, and we found out Pam was pregnant with number 3. My parents had already threatened to call social services to have our first two children removed from our custody because we weren't giving them meat or sugar, so we knew that telling them of a third child would not go over well, so we decided to run.

By now Josh was old enough that he should be starting school, but we didn't want to put him in public school. Our faith in pretty much ALL of the institutions of America was slim at best, and we were seeking a different kind of learning environment for our children. That's when we discovered, with the help of some friends, Lotus Land School in Archer, Florida.

Archer was a very small village then, about halfway between Gainesville and Cedar Key on the Gulf coast. Without any means to speak of, two children, pregnant, in our Volkswagen bus, we left Blythewood for Florida and more of the Great Unknown. We let no one know where we had gone, and just disappeared for a couple of years.

April 17, 2022

Happy Easter everyone. In whatever your tradition or belief system, welcome Spring, Rebirth, Resurrection, or new beginnings. We are all Blessed to Be Here Now. There have been many transitions in my life since Pam's passing. Pam used to say, "The Soul Train is passing through, and so many are jumping on board." Relatives and old friends appear to be passing from this life faster and faster. Maybe that's because I'm getting older, or maybe that's just the way it always has been, and I'm just noticing it more now that Pam has made her frequency hop. I can tell that the Earth is moving, and the seasons transitioning because the full moon doesn't shine on her side of the bed in the morning like it did a month ago. The Heavens and Earth are moving....always. Hold on.

We found Archer, Florida, and Lotus Land School through contact with some old friends, and arrived in our micro bus with two children, pregnant Pam, with little money and no employment. It just seemed like the right thing to do at the time. Run away and find a fresh place where life would be different. Lotus Land was a "hippie" school run by a young Jewish couple in a very rural setting on a small sand road with gigantic live oak trees and Spanish moss. It was in a converted house and had an athletic field and small playground. There were all kinds of animals there. It was not a working farm, but the animals there were mostly for the students to be able to learn about interactions with animals.

There were chickens, geese, goats, dogs, cats, and most spectacularly peacocks with their rainbow spreading tails. We interviewed one of the teachers there and the owners, and just fell in love with their passion for children and a free learning environment. It had to be right, this was amazing.

We began looking for a house and a job. First I found a construction job with a large construction company building apartment complexes primarily for student housing at the University of Florida in Gainesville. With some money coming in, we found a house on High Street. Yes that's really the name of the street and the irony was not lost on us at the time. There were two large camphor trees outside the front door that were perfect for climbing, a large yard, and it was right beside an active rail line.

The trains came through fast and loud, but we got used to the sounds quickly. Oddly, it was almost comforting to hear the trains come by regularly. We were nervous about the proximity of the tracks and our young boys playing outside, so there was much discussion and warnings about not going near the train tracks.

Pam's pregnancy was progressing rapidly, and this was a different one. We were pretty strict vegetarians, and almost completely raw foodists, with a lot of sprouts, wheatgrass juice, fruits and vegetables and central Florida was a great place for that type of diet. There were lots of other raw foodies in the area and Gainesville had a fantastic Co-op store.

In this pregnancy, Pam only gained 12 pounds, and when Buddy was born, he weighed around 8 pounds. After the birth, she slipped right back into her skinny jeans. This was a big deal to her.

When she first realized she was pregnant, she said that she did not want a hospital birth, that she wanted a home birth, preferably with a midwife attending. We had heard there were many midwives in the Gainesville area so we started interviewing as many as we could, but could not find one that fit. In all of her pregnancies, as well as most of her life, Pam would mind map the experience well in advance. In the case of childbirth, she would begin to visualize a quick, easy labor, and a smooth healthy birth. We never found a midwife, but we found a lady who wanted to be a midwife, and we bonded with her and her husband quickly. Pam was getting her birthing kit together, and teaching Josh and Jesse what to do if she went into labor with just them there. They were only 6 and 3, but they were good students and learned a lot about childbirth.

Lotus Land had a small school bus that was painted wildly purple with pictures of animals and peacocks on the sides. It was not like the traditional yellow school buses and was easy to spot. Each year, the bus and the children would be a feature in the Gainesville Christmas Parade. Since I was working every day now, Pam would often help out at school.

The day of the parade, she had driven into town with some of the kids, and then joined the rest of the kids on the bus to ride in the parade. At the end of the parade, she and our kids got off the bus to get in our car for the ride home. It was then she realized she had left her purse with the car keys on the bus, so she ran down the street for a couple of blocks chasing the bus. She was 9 months pregnant. She got to the bus, got her purse, and went back to the car.

When I got off work, we were meeting to have dinner. She didn't feel much like eating, and the only thing she wanted was mashed potatoes, which she picked at, but did not eat. I thought we should go see our "midwife" since we were within 3 weeks of the due date. As soon as the midwife opened the door she said, "Pam, you're in labor!!!" Pam said, "What?" and she said, "Look at your belly." It was in active labor, and you could see it spasm up into a large ball, almost pointy.

Holy smokes, this was early. So we went to the house, and luckily the kids went to sleep quickly. The birth was in our bedroom, with only candles for light. It was quick, and very bloody, and Bud was born wearing the placenta like a little tam hat. The placenta had detached I guess from the bus chase. Buddy was long, and blue, and was not breathing.

We rubbed his little arms and legs and talked to him, and Pam gently breathed into his face a couple of times, and then he finally took a breath. It was the most amazing thing. As he began to breathe, he opened his eyes. Newborns are not supposed to be able to focus for the first few weeks, but he looked so intensely into our eyes, and he could focus, and had the look of an old man who was confused about where he was.

He very deliberately and slowly looked around the room at each of the four of us, making long, solid eye contact with each of us in the candle light. After all four of us had been examined, he closed his eyes and went to sleep. When he woke up he could not focus, the old man was gone, and there was a new life. I've been at quite a few births since then, but I've never seen anything like that again. I guess this experience was because of the premature nature of his birth.

The next day he was yellow. Very yellow. We took him into the medical clinic where Pam had been receiving prenatal care, and they were kind of weird. They told her this was dangerous and said they might have to do a blood transfusion and a bunch of other scary stuff.

We also had a friend who was a new doctor, so we went to see him. He said, "Oh that's bullshit, since he's early, his liver isn't quite working up to par yet. Just give him lots of fluids and put him in the sunlight a lot to help get rid of the bilirubin, and he'll be fine." That's what we did, and in a couple of days he was a lovely pink very healthy active baby.

We kept going back to the clinic for checkups, but our confidence level in the general medical community dropped significantly. So now there were 5 of us. Three children is much more intense than two. We were now outnumbered.

As always, our house was a hive of activity with many people passing through and visiting. Some began to camp in the yard. By Spring it was getting crowded, and some of them weren't leaving. I got laid off from my job, and there were too many people at the house.

An old friend called up one day and asked if we would be willing to house sit for him while they went on a trip. The house was in Key West. So, we quietly packed up, and left for Key West. I don't know how long it was before some of the campers and houseguests realized that we were gone, but it no longer mattered to us. Hallelujah!! Key West!! Clear blue water, warm wind, music everywhere. Key West in those days was a pirate town and just the place for our family for a while.

April 19, 2022

As we left Archer for Key West, we abandoned our micro bus. She had developed many mechanical issues and was just no longer reliable. Now we had a pickup truck with a homemade camper cover on the back. Oddly enough, it was quite comfortable. The older two boys rode in the back, while the youngest stayed in front with us while he was still nursing.

Those were still the days of no seatbelts, and you didn't get arrested for allowing children to ride in the back of a pickup truck. The familiarity of the Keys Highway was invigorating and wonderful. We had been to Key West years before to visit and found it welcoming and refreshingly not normal. It still had a small town atmosphere, where in a short time it seemed like everyone who lived there knew everyone else. If I remember correctly there were only 10,000 residents in the "off season." Somewhere around Thanksgiving, the population swelled to 100,000 or so for the winter. I haven't been back in a long time now, but I understand it's quite different.

We were welcomed by our friends who had asked us to house sit. Their plans were to be gone for about six months, which turned out to be longer than that. We settled in and began the obligatory visits to the beach at sunrise, to be out of the sun by ten o'clock. I watched many a tourist become lobster red by staying out during the "cancer rays" part of the day.

We played a lot of music. Key West was the kind of place where you could actually make some money by playing. Some nights were folk music, some nights were

Reggae, some were Rock, and some were Country. It really didn't matter; it was all music.

I thought it would be a good idea to go back to school, so I started a Marine Biology program at the local community college, still using my GI Bill school benefits. It was more difficult than I thought to support 3 children, play music, and go to school, but it was working...sort of. The paperwork for my registration was somehow messed up by the spelling of my name, and I never received any money. In the beginning, it didn't matter, we were just making it, because we didn't have to pay rent.

We were getting quite settled, but when the owners came back, we weren't sure where we were going to go. We hadn't thought that through. A man who often came to see us play told us that he had bought a small house beside the Key West Lighthouse, and we were welcome to come live there with him.

This was kind of a replay of earlier days. We moved in, but within a week he said this was just not going to work. So....with no place to live, and the VA not sending any money, we began to pack up the truck preparing to go north.

As we were packing, this man two houses up from us was on the porch and yelled down to us. He said he thought we were just moving in. We explained what was happening and he asked us to come up on the porch, smoke a joint, and talk awhile. We did, and this man became one of our lifelong closest friends. The man in the white hat. He was Filipino American, as if that mattered, but a gentle, sweet man. We talked for a while on the porch, and then he said, "Why don't you just move in here with me. I live here alone, and I don't mind kids."

As usual in our lives, it seemed like a good thing to do at the time. This turned out to be one of the best decisions we ever made. It didn't solve all our problems, but it sure was a blessing. We became a family.

There was this huge commercial kitchen stove, and Pam really started to use it. She loved that stove, and for many years afterward she would refer back to that as the best stove she ever had. We were directly across the street from the Hemingway house and had frequent visits from the cats with six toes.

We started doing Sunday pancake breakfasts for a lot of the locals, and street people. Word got out, and there would be a regular crowd in the back yard, with Pam sending out pancakes as fast as she could make them, and afterward we would play music, and everyone would sing. It was like a Key West church service. Communion was pancakes and wine was always there, and weed as well. It was fellowship and service at its best. No expectations of donations, but somehow there was always enough to go around. Kind of like the loaves and the fishes. There was definitely a feeling of spiritual closeness and brother/sisterhood. Love always finds a way.

Winter came, if you can call it that in Key West, Christmas came and went, and we were happy. But the VA was still failing to send money, and we were starting to really struggle financially. Near the end of the winter quarter, we realized we couldn't keep this up. We were supplementing the no income with construction work when it was there, but it was becoming unworkable.

We began to realize that we were going to have to leave and go north and find a job. So, we put the boys in the back of the truck and began the trip back to South Carolina where we had family, friends, and the possibility of work. It was a sad and painful thing to leave our dear friend and the fellowship of the Key West community, but we didn't see any other possibilities. It had been wonderful while it lasted.

We made our way up, and stopped to visit my parents who were glad to see us after disappearing for a few years. We had slowly begun to open lines of communication with them after a two year no talking period and the disappearance. It was great to talk to them and see them again.

I still didn't know what I was going to do about work, but at least I was now in a familiar environment. Still no money from the VA for the 9 months of school attendance. I know it seems crazy, but those funds had factored heavily in our budget and the failure to receive anything had left us without any money, and off center. Any planning that we had collapsed.

We didn't want to stay with my parents, and everything seemed kind of bleak. Then we found the BIG bus! A 66 passenger 1957 Chevrolet school bus. The owner had purchased it with the thought of converting it to a camper, and had collected some equipment for the bus, but had not done much with it. He had a small gas cook stove, a small ammonia refrigerator and a few other items. They were just sitting inside an empty bus. There were still some seats, but mostly it was empty.

It had been in service as a church bus, and still had the sign for Dutch Fork Baptist Church on the side.

I could see great potential in this vehicle. I had worked on sailboats and done a lot of construction work, and I could see the possibility of a comfortable home inside this bus....with a lot of work. If we gathered together all the money we had left, and sold the truck, we would have just enough money to buy the bus.

Pam always loved living in vehicles, from the hearse, the VW bug, the VW bus, and the truck/camper. There was always some level of freedom when you could live in your vehicle. There were the lyrics to a song, "There's nothing like a hundred miles between me and trouble in my mind. Nothing like a hundred miles when you're only passing through. Nothing like a hundred miles to make me forget about you." We did it. Another leap of faith. The big jump. The edge of the ledge.

My parents were completely freaked out! They thought we were going to finally settle down in a little house and I would get a regular job and life would be normal. Normal was just not in our vocabulary. We left Columbia in a snowstorm, in an empty bus with some kitchen gear, very,

very little money left, and a feeling of excitement, exhilaration, and hope.

A dense fog came in with the snow, and as we went along the interstate highway, visibility was next to zero. Big trucks would appear in the fog to pass us like some great whale coming out of the unseen depths, only to disappear again in the fog ahead of us. We had no idea of where we were going, but we were on our way again and that was somehow comforting.

April 20, 2022

We had a saying after that escape in the fog. "Onward through the fog." We used that often, even shortly before her death.

There was no particular direction we were going, just Onward through the fog. Frequently we would go to the end of the driveway, or where ever we were and look at each other and say, "Right or Left?" and just make a split second decision to go one way or the other and the adventure would begin. Furthermore, we would often arrive someplace just in the nick of time for some unexpected experience that was always perfect.

On this first trip, the bus was empty inside, with just the few loose appliances and a few seats. A big open space. It was clean and we put a big mattress down for sleeping. In those days we had what we called the family bed, and Pam and I and all 3 children slept in the same bed. It was cozy, and there was always lots of reading out loud at bedtime, because there was no TV or radio or even any kind of music device except my guitar and our voices. But there was lots of music and singing.

Our first stop was at a friend's house in mid South Carolina, where I had a short term construction job, and there were lots of construction scraps, like odd plywood pieces, and lumber. In the off hours, I began to build our home inside the bus. I had done a pretty good bit of sailboat work and had the skills to build inside of a vehicle. In fact, while we were in Key West, we met quite a few "boat people." People who lived on sailboats, and just traveled around with their families.

One particular single woman had 3 children of her own, and 2 adopted children, and they seemed quite happy and well adjusted. The children were so nice and were good play companions for our kids. Mostly at the beach. We thought we would like to do this, but I knew there were many skills and downsizing that we would have to do to be actually living on a boat.

The bus was the next best thing. We figured if we could get good at living in the tube of the bus, we could eventually make that tube a boat. Some of the things about living in a vehicle: 1. Everything that you have must have a secure place and must be multifunctional. 2. If you are going to get something new, something old must go. There is only so much space. 3. Anything not on board when we leave is no longer part of our lives.

I built a very pleasant and comfortable home inside the bus. There were bunks for the two older boys, which also served as sofa type seats near the front of the bus, and a large king size bed in the back for Pam, the youngest, and me.

There was a really nice kitchen with ample counter space, a stainless sink, a small ammonia refrigerator, and a small gas cook stove with oven. Shelves ran along the whole bus above the windows with straps to secure everything while moving. There was a lot of storage under the counters, bunks, beds, and I even built some storage underneath the bus, accessible from the outside.

The driver's seat was large and comfortable like a captain's chair from a boat and had room enough so that while we were traveling, the driver could get up and move around one side of the seat while the next driver could move in place, all without stopping. It made long journeys so much easier because we could swap out driving without having to stop at all, and the previous driver could sleep, or fix something to eat while continuing to move. Sailboats and buses don't move fast, but they move steadily.

The bus did not have cruise control, but it did have a throttle that could be set, allowing the bus to maintain a steady speed without tiring your foot. Water was carried in 3 five-gallon glass water containers, and there were special trays made for growing sprouts. All kinds of sprouts, which is mostly what we ate. The sprouts would grow in the trays, and when we were parked, we would move them to the roof for sunlight and green them up. We even grew some vegetables that way. It was like having a garden on the road. She was a sweet ride, and Pam often said that it was her favorite home. Shortly before her passing, she wanted to see if we could find her again and get her back.

After some mechanical work, and finishing the interior, we were ready to "set sail."

For the next few years, we traveled. When people asked where we were from, we would always say the 51st state, the interstate. Having spent some time with Native Americans, we had accepted the belief that land was not to be owned, and we belonged to the land, not the other way around, so we would also tell people that we lived on the lines between properties and states.

I worked a lot of construction jobs, and we played a lot of music. The bus made it possible to pull up to the stage doors and hang out with our children, make dinner, and just go out and perform, and in the breaks, step back into our home. We often had friends caring for the children while we were on stage, but the kids also frequently slept in guitar cases backstage until we finished playing and moved them to their beds, and on to the next stop.

We spent a lot of this time near the ocean in Florida, and in the South. Warm weather is your friend when you live in a bus, and proximity to the ocean was an absolute necessity for health. We had one particular stop in Miami where a friend was living in the last private residence on Miami Beach.

All the area for at least a quarter mile north of their house had been cleared of homes and was just dunes and beach brush waiting to be developed. We were able to park next to the house in this cleared area, with the permission of the police. The front wheels of the bus sat on Miami Beach. At night there were boats that dropped off immigrants in the dark. Mostly from Haiti I think. Often, the refugees would come up and sleep under the bus to get out of the rain and then slip away into Miami before daylight.

We have lived most of our lives with poor people, immigrants, refugees, prisoners, outlaws, and castaways. They have always been wonderful companions on the crazy journey we have been on. It was not lost on me that the really wealthy people that we were around with my uncle and the elite crowd never seemed happy, and they were always selfish, protecting whatever they valued, while the poorest were always willing to share whatever little they had, and in the darkest times they always seemed to find happiness and song. They made me feel sacred and human.

April 21, 2022

There are so many stories of life on the road and the bus, some happy, some sad, some exciting, and some just average days and nights, but never boring. I cannot tell you the number of times we left with no particular place to go, and arrived to a warm welcome from people who would tell us we were just in time, they had been waiting for us. A recording was under way and it was time for our parts. We would literally arrive, park the bus, and go into the studio.

Never any planning, just Be Here Now. There was a wonderful woman, Becky Johnson, who had land in the sandhill pines outside of Columbia who always welcomed us, and we had a quiet, private place we could park the bus for days or weeks if we wanted. There was a large pond where we and the children could swim and they learned to fish.

Her son Mark was just a young, rowdy teenager when we met him, and he became one of our best friends. He lived in the "Bunk House," and we spent a lot of time talking, eating, and playing together. He had built a tight rope for practicing balance, and it was excellent exercise for the children as well.

This was kind of our refuge when the road got too tiring. Becky was a powerful force in the local politics and protected us from those who wanted to have us investigated by social services. Except for a brief trial with a Montessori school, and our periods at Lotus Land, we home schooled all of our children, and there were always those in the communities that thought that was wrong.

Our ideas for education came from our own experience and reading John Holt's ideas for learning. I'm not going to go into all of that, you can read about that on your own. Our belief was that children were much more intelligent and curious than anyone thought. We thought that they were born curious and had great capacity for learning that sometimes took 12 years of traditional school to destroy.

We felt that reading was absolutely essential, so all of our children could read very well before they were six years old. After learning to read, library skills were the next step. In those days, there was no Google, or "devices" for reading or researching, there was the library and card catalog, and the other resources for inquiring minds. And by library skills, I mean being able to use the facility well to explore any subject that you were curious about.

Wherever we went, one of the first things we did was get library cards for all of us and begin checking out books on each of our interests. There was a point early on where Josh had read almost every book in the Richland County Children's library, and had begun his foray into the adult library before he was 7.

It was common for each of our children to read 10 books a week, and us as well. That would later mean checking out 60 books a week from the Library Truck. We were very popular with librarians. Once the kids could read well, and knew their way around the library, general math skills were important, so we spent time on that. We felt that after they knew how to read, write and find their way to the information that interested them, that our job was to help them with whatever they were interested in, and let their natural curiosity carry them wherever their particular talents would lead them.

Whenever we reached a level where they passed our knowledge of a subject, we encouraged them to write to the authors of the latest books on their current interest, and tell the author what they already knew, and ask questions of what to do next. They almost always got wonderful responses from really famous authors with supreme guidance.

There was always the nighttime family reading of a particular series or book. Sometimes we did listen to audio recordings of books as well as a family activity. I am proud to say that I read The Hobbit, and The Lord Of The Rings trilogy out loud to every one of my children, usually with the older kids sitting in and adding their impressions of the tales. By the way, they were not the only books I read to them.

Later on, when we were forced to send Josh and Jesse to public school, they had to be tested for class placement. At the time they were 11 and 8, and they both tested at second year college reading levels, and the local school principal didn't know what to do. That's for a later part of the story.

The First 60 Days

One of our favorite children's authors was Shel Silverstein. Yep, the same one who wrote for Playboy Magazine. He wrote some wonderful children's books and they were popular with all of our boys. One day while we were parked on the street in Key West in the big bus, Shel was passing by, and looked in the window. He was easily recognized.

He came up to the front door of the bus and asked if he could come aboard. The whole family was so excited so all of us welcomed him in. He spent the whole afternoon hanging out with us and asking lots of questions about our lives, and what we were doing. Obviously some of his books were out on the reading space. It was a fabulous encounter and left us feeling so much better about our crazy life and situation. Just to have someone recognize what we were doing and give us encouragement instead of criticism. There were many other encounters like this with people both famous and not so famous. That night we opened for Ritchie Havens in Key West.

Everything was cosmic and wonderful until our engine blew up outside of Archer, Florida. We had thrown a rod, and the engine was completely ruined. As with everything else in our lives, there was perfection even in this.

We were just a few miles from Lotus Land School, and we flagged down the sewer pump out truck. We knew the driver from our past times in Archer. He towed us to the edge of the woods behind the athletic field at Lotus Land. As it turned out, they needed a bus driver for the beginning session of school, and I was a perfect candidate. So, in exchange for driving their school bus, we were allowed to stay in the bus and our kids could go to school. Oh, did I mention Pam was pregnant with number 4.

April 22, 2022

That winter in the field at Lotus Land was stressful, but wonderful also. Pam had a red string bikini and would often ride her bicycle a couple of miles into Archer to get water and groceries. Aside from the bus, we had no transportation except bicycles.

It was a relatively quiet time, except for all the school kids who loved to come visit in the bus and play nearby. When you live in any type of vehicle, whether it's a boat, or a car, or a bus, you must become skilled at mechanics. There is always something failing, and if you don't have the money to continually take it to the shop, you learn to do the repairs yourself.

A good friend, John Fitzgerald in Archer brought me some scaffolding and a chain hoist, and I was able to remove the old broken engine, disassemble it, and see what had failed and if it was salvageable. There was a broken connecting rod which had collided with the crankshaft and had made a dimple in one of the rod journals on the crankshaft. Maybe that's too much information...anyway, it was broken and would take a significant amount of work and parts to repair.

I had seen another motor like this at some friends in South Carolina that was in working condition but not in service, so I called to see if I could get it. They agreed, and John and I took off for South Carolina in his modified Oldsmobile 88 and retrieved the engine. While I was there, I managed to get a couple of days construction work, which gave me a little bit of money.

We returned to Archer, and I installed the new engine in the bus. With my job driving the Lotus Land bus, and other odd jobs, getting and replacing the engine had taken several months. But, the engine was in, and came to life. This enabled us to charge the batteries and do a few other checkout chores. In the meantime, Pam was getting more and more pregnant, with large belly, but still wearing the red string bikini. She was never ashamed of her body, and always proud of the beauty of pregnancy. Actually, I think a pregnant woman is the most beautiful thing on earth.

It was our good fortune again that there were two midwives in the area who were members of The Farm in Tennessee. For those of you who don't know, The Farm was a commune of hippies who traveled from San Francisco in a 250 school bus caravan to Summertown, Tennessee and were led by Stephen Gaskin. His wife Ina May Gaskin was instrumental in reviving midwifery in the United States and created a school for midwives. She has been described as "the mother of modern midwifery" and developed the Gaskin Maneuver, which came in handy with the birth of our fourth son. Anyway, two of the midwives from The Farm assisted us with the birth of Willie, in the bus. I'll tell you more about this later.

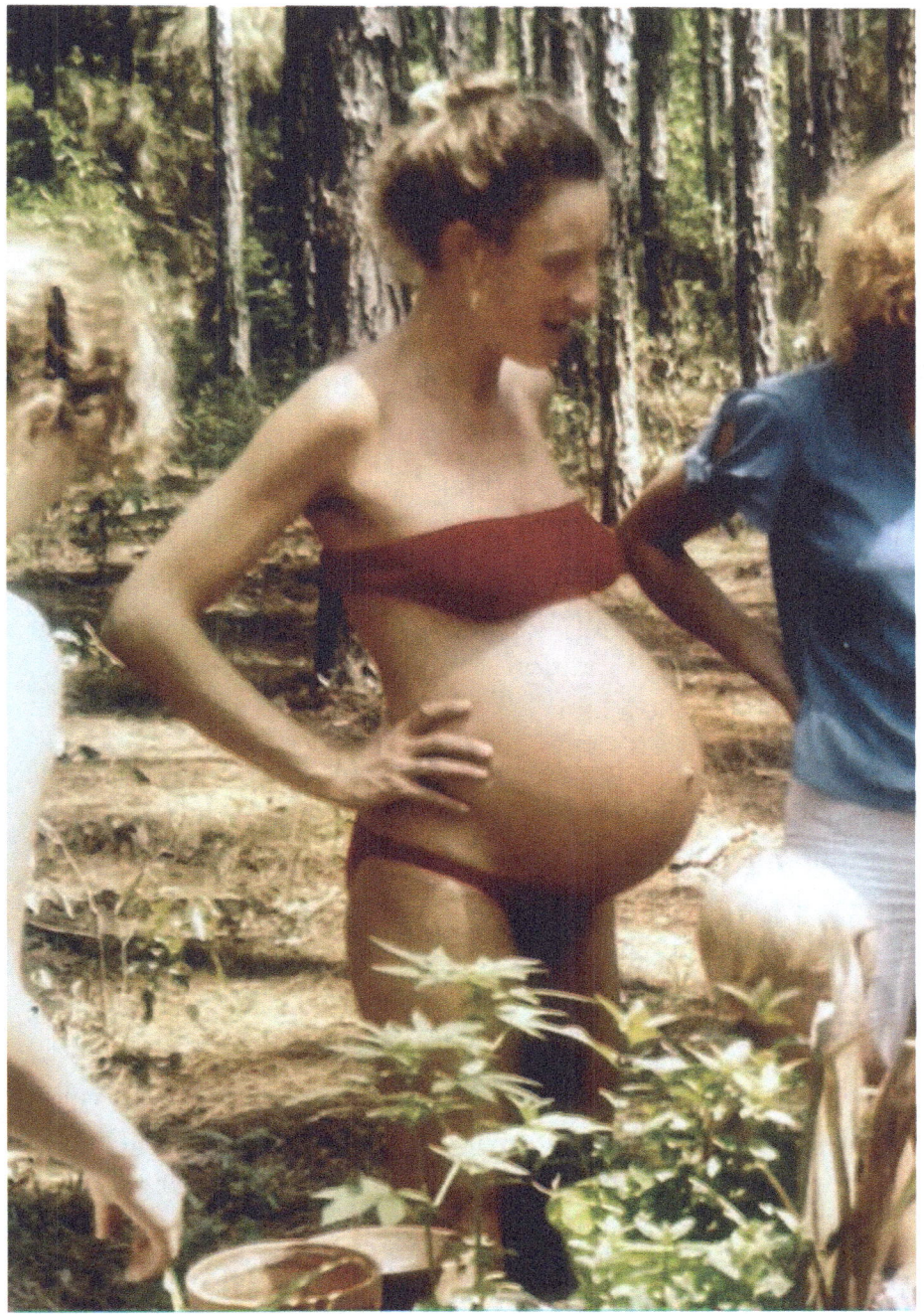

We took the bus on several short trips with the "new" engine, just to keep everything loose, and check the engine out to be sure it was working properly. We were starting to run short of money again, because I had broken a bone in my wrist while chaperoning the Lotus Land kids at a skating rink and couldn't do any construction work.

A pot grower friend of ours near Tallahassee let us know he had some weed that we could get if we wanted to sell it. I want to emphasize that we were never in the business of dealing any type of drugs, but this would enable us to get through the winter by trading for some goods.

On Christmas Eve, 1980, we left Lotus Land for Tallahassee to retrieve a large construction size bag of weed. I put our last $25 into the gas tank of the bus, and off we went. About halfway to Tallahassee, the bus started to develop a strange vibration. I pulled over onto the shoulder of the road to take a look.

I had developed a technique for pulling the transmission from inside the bus and set about doing that to troubleshoot where the vibration was coming from. Long story short, the driveshaft on the new engine had broken in two. I could still start the bus, but I couldn't put any stress on the engine without risk of catastrophic failure.

We were in a part of Florida that was flat farmland, and the roadbed was the highest point around. It was very cold, and the wind was blowing fiercely across the flats and hitting the bus broadside. At one point, I was under the bus working on the engine when a Highway Patrolman stopped to see if we were okay. I told him what was happening, and he said he would check on us later. We never saw him again.

I was in pretty significant pain from the broken wrist and working on the engine, and the temperature was dropping. It was unusually cold, dropping into the upper 20's, with this unrelenting wind. It was getting cold on the bus, and there was absolutely no traffic at all, you know it was Christmas Eve.

Pam walked about a half mile up to a farmhouse to make a phone call and got our friends in Tallahassee who said they could get to us the next day, with a truck and see if they could tow us back to Lotus Land.

It was a very cold and lonely night, and I couldn't get the Christmas story of Jesus's birth out of my mind. All five of us snuggled in the big bed, and reading stories by candlelight, while Pam and I waited for sunrise and some level of warmth.

Early the next morning, sure enough, they showed up with a pickup truck, chains, and a big, big bag of weed. I wasn't sure this little truck could pull the bus, but if I started the bus and got it moving, the little truck could make it. After an extremely intense tow trip, we landed back at our old spot in the Lotus Land field on Christmas morning with zero money, but a big, big bag of weed under the bed, and we were all still alive, and together. Merry Christmas everybody.

April 23, 2022

I wonder if there will ever be a time when I don't wake up marking time by thinking how long it has been since she breathed. This is my new life.

When we returned to Lotus Land in our newly disabled condition, I knew we were kind of screwed. Now we had no money at all, the bus wasn't completely dead, but it was clear that it was not going anywhere in the near future. I could still crank her up for a while to charge the batteries and keep our 12 volt electrical system operating so we had lights and a couple of 12 volt accessories to keep us going as long as that last 25 dollars' worth of gas that I had put in would hold out in short bursts. I was still driving the Lotus Land bus each morning, and occasionally picking up some local construction work, and periodically selling some of that big, big bag of weed, but it was tough times.

It was now the middle of winter, and sometimes the nights were cold, but it was Florida after all, so most days were sunny and warm. Pam was moving along in her pregnancy with a due date in April, but she was still riding that bicycle in her red string bikini most days. Somehow, we still laughed a lot each day, played music at night, had lots of friends stopping by to sing and play as well, so it wasn't all dark. And best of all, at the end of the day our family was all together, still eating (now on food stamps), and reading to each other at night.

We had faith that somehow, someway, it was going to work out if we kept holding on to The Dream. Like Don Quixote we still believed in The Dream and continuing that Glorious Quest and that Love will conquer all. Without the knight of mirrors we knew we were invincible. I actually can't imagine how our situation must have looked to someone on the outside. Inside it all, we were still happy.

There was a point, as there always is, when the darkness got shorter, the days got longer, and the birth of our fourth son was approaching. I had been steadily working on a solution to the engine repair and was near to her resurrection. In the very early morning of April 30th, Pam went into active labor. We could get to a phone inside the school, and contacted the midwives who arrived very quickly, as they knew Pam's history of quick deliveries.

There was a beautiful peach colored full moon in the sky, and the outside world looked ethereal in that light, while inside the bus, everything was warmly glowing with candle lights.

As the labor became more active, the other boys woke up, and each was given a job to assist Pam in the process. One was to hold her hand, one was to get ice chips to ease her dry mouth, and another was to pass supplies to the midwives. Our children knew where babies come from. Truth was always important to us, messy as it sometimes is.

Willie's birth was not quite as easy as the other three. He was not long and thin; he was short and stocky, and his shoulders were so broad that he was having difficulty getting through the birth canal. In the hospital they would probably have moved to cesarean surgery at this point, but the midwives just oiled her up with olive oil, and gently reached in and turned him slightly and eased him out. Remember how I said something earlier about the Gaskin Maneuver? This was it, and it worked! I cut the umbilical cord, and now we were six.

He was healthy and beautiful in the candle/full moon light. The other boys were so excited to have another brother, and we were relieved and ecstatic at the new life in our family. It was so magical we almost named him Peach Moon, but fortunately we were grounded enough not to saddle him with that. William David Holder McMahon. His name contained both of his grandfather's names, and Pam's father's last name Holder, so he would know his lineage. But to us he was and is to this day, Willie D.

The boys made a big banner for the front of the bus saying "IT'S A BOY!" and as the students arrived, there was a steady procession to view the new addition through the bus window.

Not long after that, Pam reminded me that my father was one of eight boys, and we had four, and she wasn't going any further down this road. She said, "Donald T, you're going to have to cut that thing off." Later I would have a vasectomy out of some level of good conscience, and knowing there would be no more love making without assurance of no more pregnancies. We knew our family was complete. We often joked that our potential for fertilization was so high, that all we had to do was pass by each other and BAM she was pregnant again.

The bus engine was also beginning its breath of life again. The repairs that I had made to the engine were complete, and miraculously she was vibrant and ready to move. When we would get out on the road, the feeling of freedom was exhilarating and we could feel changes in the air. Just to be able to move lifted our spirits.

We still had no idea where we would go, or what the next step would be, but we knew something was happening. New life in the family and new life in the journey.

The First 60 Days

At the end of the school year, we took the bus on a short trip to see our friend Julian who lived out in the sand flats and shallow ponds of Watermelon Pond, far out in the country outside of Archer. It was a beautiful place of white sand, short oak trees, and many clear, shallow, spring fed ponds. There were gopher tortoises, rattlesnakes, and alligators, all of which seemed like good neighbors if you left them alone and just acknowledged that this was their home, and we were just visiting. Awake and aware were the keywords.

After a short visit with Julian, we decided to try the bus out on a longer trip, so we started in a northward direction to visit with Becky Johnson and see our old good friend Mark. He was building a sailboat to go cruising the Caribbean and we wanted to see them, as well as check out the boat.

We had been getting letters from some friends in Hawaii telling us that we needed to come there. That it was beautiful, and there were mountains and the ocean, and the weather was always good. We had reached a point in our dietary exploration where we were fully raw foodists, with no meat or dairy, and we fasted at least one day a week. We had lost all body fat, and actually were highly energized and physically felt the best we had ever felt in our lives.

One issue with getting your body so clean and lean is that you have to live in a clean environment, or the smallest contamination affects your health. Florida was not, and certainly not the South in general, clean enough for us now. There was too much air pollution, and even the water at the coast was being contaminated by industrialization and development. A lot of the places that we used to go that were pristine were now being rapidly developed with condos and golf courses. We could see that we needed a cleaner environment. Hawaii was sounding pretty good, and our friends assured us that there were possibilities of houses and work.

So, I took on a rebuilding project that would take a couple of months, and Pam decided to sell her engagement ring from her first marriage to get enough money to get plane tickets to Hawaii. This was going to be a BIG jump and was kind of scary. So......with one-way plane tickets, and $1500 in cash, we left the bus with Mark, and climbed on a plane to Hilo, Hawaii.

We left Columbia just before sunrise and saw 3 separate sunrises on the way to Hawaii. It was Jesse's birthday, and he was feeling sick. We made that trip with Jesse having a fever and not feeling well. It was long, and by the time we landed in Hilo, it was the afternoon of the same day we had left, but it felt like two days later.

All the passengers on the plane deboarded while we sat and waited with Jesse still not feeling well. Our friends who were meeting us to pick us up almost left, thinking that we had backed out. But we managed to get off the plane in time to catch them, got in their jeep, and went to a small motel/cabin for the night, and completely crashed out and slept soundly until the next morning.

By daylight, Jesse was feeling much better, and we were somewhat rested, and climbed into the jeep for the trip over the volcano to the Kona side. This was definitely not Kansas anymore, and the next big experience was unfolding all around us.

The First 60 Days

April 24, 2022

Hawaii. There are not enough words in the English language to adequately describe Hawaii. I think the word awe was invented for this place. No photographs or descriptions ever captured what it's like to actually be present and feel the power of standing on an active volcano. AWESOME.

That first night, we all slept in the same room on pallets on the floor. We were so exhausted that we could have slept on the rocks outside and would still have rested well. When I opened the door of our room, there in front of me was Mauna Kea in all her glory rising 14,000 feet into the crystal blue sky. It was such a clear day, that I could see the observatories on the peak.

The air was warm and humid, and tropical plants of all kinds were everywhere. Surely this was paradise. I am always the early riser, so it was a while before anyone else woke up. I just stood outside in wonder. I had never seen anything like this before. After a bit, everyone was up and moving, and we had breakfast and loaded up for the trip to the Kona side.

The Big Island is about 250 miles around on the main highway, and roughly 100 miles from Hilo to Kona. Nothing prepares you for that ride. We were all packed into a Toyota Land Cruiser with a little trailer for our luggage. We brought everything we had pretty much, which was a lot more than we needed, but we had no idea of what we might need there, and in those days there basically was no baggage limit on the airlines.

The First 60 Days

The first place they took us was a spot to get in the ocean. Oh my, the Pacific. Hawaii is almost 3,000 miles out in the Pacific from Los Angeles, and the flight time is about 6 hours. I remember thinking when we were flying across all that water, and landing on what, from the air, seemed like a small island, that we were waaaaay out here, and if something happened, we couldn't drive away. The only way back from here was in the air or the water. I felt a little nervous as well as excited.

When my feet touched the water of the Pacific, my first reaction was, "Holy crap, this water is cold!" Back in Key West, the water was so warm that most of the time you could stay out snorkeling for hours and it was so warm and pleasant that it felt like a bath, but this water felt really cold to be in the tropics.

Oh well, we moved back into the jeep and headed on to Kona. We very quickly left the city of Hilo and started through jungle terrain, and soon came into the view of Kīlauea. It was dormant at that time and had been dormant for an unusually long period.

In those days, there was a road that wound its way up the face of the volcano. I don't think that road exists anymore, but it was like a small, rough road with a lot of switchbacks. It felt like going up the side of a 4,000 foot black teacup that had black spills all over the sides. It was one of the first times I felt exceptionally small and insignificant in the Universe. "This is so BIG" is all I could think of. Also, everything that wasn't green, was black lava of various forms.

When we reached the summit, we stopped to have lunch, and I had time to walk over and look at the caldera. It was about a mile across and looked like a flat, black solid lake, with little bits of steam. I climbed down and very lightly walked on it. It was warm through my shoes, and made me feel queasy, so I quickly climbed back up to the rest of the family.

That lunch was the first time I had eaten green coconuts. I loved them. We made little spoons out of the coconut husks to scoop out the jellied flesh inside.

The main road that circumnavigates the island is about 1500 feet in elevation, and everywhere you go, you can see the Pacific stretched out below, with the green of the jungle rising above. The green was periodically scarred by prior lava flows, reminding you that these mountains were still very much alive.

By late afternoon, we finally reached Captain Cook and the little house of our friends. We slept in the open air on the porch that night. The constant gentle breeze made such comforting whispering sounds through the banana leaves. The next day we set up our tent in the jungle behind our friend's house and began to look for more permanent housing and work.

Within a few days, we were introduced to an amazing woman who had a coffee lease up the mountain and was getting ready to leave for an extended trip to the mainland and was looking for someone to stay in the house, and work the coffee trees, which were nearing picking time. What a fortuitous meeting.

This woman was a powerhouse of political influence on the Big Island and an advocate for women's rights. She and Pam hit it off immediately, and it was decided that this would be our next living situation. I didn't know squat about coffee farming, but I was certainly willing to try anything, and the little house up on stilts on the side of Mauna Loa was so beautiful and inviting.

She had another small living space a short walk up a steep trail where she was staying while we moved into the lower house and began to learn the ins and outs of life on a coffee farm. She had a daughter who was about Josh's age, and I don't know exactly how to describe the "man" in the relationship. He wasn't her husband, or even her significant other at that time, but they were living together, and he was a genuine experience to meet.

His name was Norman, and he was full blood Hawaiian. He had dark skin, a beard, and spoke in what seemed to me to be growls and grunts. It took a few weeks before I could actually understand what he was saying. In some ways he seemed very frightening, and at the same time gentle and kind. I had never met anyone like Norman.

The first morning when we woke up in the house there, Norman was looking in the window, and just walked in. He was smoking a big joint, which Pam immediately started sharing, while she was nursing Willie. He was looking at

Willie, and somehow we understood him to say, "Look at the eyes on this little one," and he picked Willie up from Pam's arms and walked off. Pam and I looked at each other with a startled, frightened look and wondered if this okay.

Norman disappeared into the jungle holding Willie in his arms and didn't return for a while. When they did come back, both he and Willie were laughing, and I looked in his eyes and saw genuine Love looking back from this really foreign looking human.

From that moment on, we became close and lasting friends, and Norman began to teach me the skills I would need to operate in Hawaii as a native. Neither he nor I knew we were both Vietnam veterans until many years later. That was in the period of denial of service.

My morning chores are calling, and I will have to continue this later. I Love you All.

April 27, 2022

Several people have messaged or contacted me to make sure I'm alright because I haven't posted in a couple of days. I have not been banished from Facebook, nor anything untoward, it's just that work and chores have kept me very busy for a couple of days and I just got tired. But it's nice to know that people are waiting for an episode and checking on me.

Jackie and Norman stayed for a couple of weeks to show us what we needed to do to maintain the coffee farm, and the house while they were gone. As I said earlier, Norman was teaching me Hawaiian skills of farming and life in general. He was a great and funny teacher.

In the beginning I had difficulty understanding his manner of speaking with his grunts, growls, and pidgin English, but I learned and adapted quickly. I was used to gardening and farming on the mainland from growing up in the south, and the community at Brown Earth. I even did a short stint at NC State University in the Agriculture Department, but none of that prepared me for Hawaii.

The piece of land that we were on was only four acres, and only a few hundred feet wide, but was vertical and steep. My first lesson was going out at sunrise and walking in the coffee land. I had only gone a few steps into the coffee trees, when I stepped on a slick lava rock and landed on my back on that same rock and caused a spasm in my back. I learned that Hawaii is beautiful and green, but also VERY hard and because of the daily rain, is VERY slippery.

The Big Island has very little actual dirt, it is all lava of various forms. I didn't even know there were different kinds of lava. There is Pahoehoe lava, which is a solid pillow type of lava that is smooth and forms as lava slowly flows, and there is aa lava which is more rough and rubbly, comes in lots of sizes from pebbles to boulders, and is usually very sharp, and there is the fine lava dust or sand that usually comes at the end of an eruption and is like fine sand of varying colors. Within those there are lots of gradations, but the point is that the whole island is lava of some form.

I developed a saying while I was there that whoever could make the most dirt wins. Jackie's was one of only a couple of farms in the valley that were attempting to go organic. I should mention here that authentic Kona coffee only comes from the Honaunau valley, and it's only 30 or 40 miles wide. A lot of the coffee farms were small leases from the Bishop Estate, and were mostly leased to people who could show some relation to native Hawaiians.

Jackie secured her lease because her husband was full blood Hawaiian, and she fought long and hard to get it. There was already a transition from Hawaiians to others. Gentrification takes many forms. Most of the hippies that were in this part of Hawaii were here to grow pot because it was a great climate for it, and very little consequence if caught.

Our friends who had encouraged us to come to Hawaii were growers, and thought that once we saw how easy it was to grow, that we would join in. We did not. We didn't want to get into the drug business in any way other than as consumers. We were there for the climate, the ocean, and the idea that we could follow our raw food diet much easier there than anywhere else. Norman watched us closely to see if we were trying to grow pot. When he became convinced that we were authentic in our purpose, so much opened up for us.

I'm finding this episode difficult to write. It's hard to explain the many facets going on. We tried to read and research as much about Hawaii as we could before we took the leap to get on that plane, but the reality was very different from anything we could grasp.

There were not that many books available on the mainland that told the story from the Hawaiian's perspective. When we got our library cards from the little Captain Cook library, we found lots of books, written by Hawaiians that told a totally different story of this land. It was a tale of brutal exploitation and theft of the islands by greedy and misguided missionaries. What we found was that the native Hawaiians, not the post card, tourist version of these people, actually didn't like white people very much.

And the hippies were just one more wave of whites taking more than they were contributing. The natives that we knew didn't care much for the business of pot, they were only interested in sharing it. They shared everything. If you came upon a case or two of beer, you didn't take it home, you shared it with your friends.

They had no real sense of time other than now. Any time other than now was bombye. This was a term derived from the missionaries who were trying to convince the natives that you were to be good now so that you would receive your reward in the sweet by and by. So bombye could mean anything from a few minutes to days. When they said they would meet you bombye, you never really knew when that would be, but they WOULD show up sometime.

After Norman decided that we were genuine, so many natives would greet us with, "Oh, you the ones stay wid Norman," and there would be much laughter and back slapping and sometimes hugging. Prior to that time, we got many sideways glances and scowls. Reading and hearing the stories from them, I could understand their skepticism of white people, and felt a sense of shame.

I don't want to stir up controversy about critical race theory, but I saw a lot here that was the same as the old South, but it was more under the surface rather than the overt racism of South Carolina. There was such beauty here, and tragedy.

Norman was so gracious. He taught me how to get the bananas from the tall Cavendish banana trees, and how to pick coffee, and so many different kinds of fruit that I had never seen before. When Jackie and Norman left for the mainland, she left us with the keys to her Volkswagen beetle so we had transportation, and we settled into a daily routine which involved picking coffee and weed eating in the morning, and then as the rain began in the late morning we would head downhill to the coast where it was always sunny and 90 degrees.

We could watch the clouds on the mountain and when it would begin to clear after lunch, we would head back up. It was just a few miles between but was like two different worlds. In fact, the Big Island was a land of microclimates. One side of the ridge got rain every day, and a half mile away it never rained. It was wonderful and terrible at the same time.

We were there for about six months before we realized that we were never going to be able to stay here for very long for a lot of reasons. The main one was employment. The only work I could find was agricultural, and that was no more than $10 and hour in a $50 an hour economy, so every hour that I worked, we went $40 further down.

Our grower friends were making hundreds of thousands of dollars which they kept in grocery bags around the house because they were afraid to spend it because of the IRS attention. We decided we would have to leave, but it would take another year to find a way to leave.

We came with one-way tickets, and getting six one-way tickets out of Hawaii is much more difficult than getting one-way tickets in. Almost all flights out of Hawaii are full of round trippers. Also, there was the matter of acquiring enough money to buy those tickets if we could find them.

We had Mark sell the big bus for us and send us the money, which we used to buy a VW bus so we would have transportation when Jackie came back, and our original $1500 was long gone. The last six months of our Hawaiian experience was in a tent in the jungle. Many people have said to us, "My God, you were homeless," and Pam would usually say, "No, we weren't homeless, we had a tent." I guess in retrospect, we did spend quite a bit of time "homeless," but we never felt that way at the time.

Donald T. McMahon

April 28, 2022

The whippoorwills and morning birds are really talking it up this morning. It's chilly, so I have a fire in the woodstove as I sit down to write this morning's episode.

For the first few weeks at Jackie's, Norman would show up shortly after daylight each morning, and take Willie away into the jungle. We really trusted Norman. By this time Pam had really settled into her weed addiction. She was smoking pretty much continuously. At night before going to bed, she would roll up three big joints and place them on the bedside table. In the morning, she would smoke one as she was getting up, one while she was cooking breakfast, and one while she was rolling three more.

She had graduated to the primo bud, which I could not even share with her, because if I smoked even a small amount of that grade of weed, I just went back to sleep, so I was smoking "shake," which is the leaves that are trimmed from the buds to make the buds a higher grade, and more valuable. Even with the shake, I couldn't come close to keeping up with her. Pam seemed to get energized from smoking, whereas I just got sleepier.

I would smoke a little before going out into the coffee land to pick and it made the day, and the work, somewhat magical. Coffee trees are amazing plants. The farm was planted on a grid, with coffee trees spaced about six feet apart, and then every 25 feet or so would be banana trees, rising above the coffee, and papayas scattered about as well, with passion fruit vines twining through some of the trees, guavas, and other fruits in various spots over the land. Even further apart were the avocado and mango trees rising still higher. It was storied agriculture.

In one spot, Norman had his taro patch, and pineapple plants. I asked Norman how you knew when the pineapples were ripe, and he said, "You'll just know." When they were ripe, you could smell them strongly when you got near the pineapple patch, and these were not the kind of pineapples you got in the store, these were white pineapples, and the size of small watermelons, and so sweet they made your teeth hurt when you ate them. There is absolutely nothing else in this world that compares to that flavor.

There was a special avocado tree near the house that had the largest avocados ever. They were bigger than Willie's head and had a small pit. They were just like several pounds of butter with a skin. Picking them was interesting because the tree was so large. One person climbed the tree and used a long picker to get the avocados, and then drop them to the person below who used a catcher's mitt to catch them because otherwise they hurt your hands. Some would fall and actually break the fiberglass roofing sheets over the bathroom.

The view from the front windows was exquisite as a great expanse of green jungle fell below, to where Captain Cook Bay was laid out like a big pond with arms of mountains wrapping around to leave a mile wide opening to the open ocean, and the view was directly west, so almost every day when the sun set, if you watched it sink into the Pacific, you would catch the "green flash" as the last rays of the sun would pass through the clear ocean water.

Almost every day would start off crystal clear, humid, and the perfect temperature. As the morning would progress, clouds would begin to form on the mountain above us, and gradually lowering until it began to sprinkle late morning. Then we would leave for the beach because soon after the sprinkle came the downpour which could last a couple of hours, sometimes so heavy that I thought the roof couldn't possibly hold that much water.

The gutters were made from six-inch PVC pipe, which fed into the 1500 gallon cistern outside the kitchen door. When it was really raining, there was a solid 6 inch flow of water from the pipe into the cistern. That was our only water supply because the Big Island has no ground water on the Kona side.

The bathroom was in a separate small room reached by a decked walkway beside the cistern, and had an actual indoor toilet, and a tub which was rare up in these jungle houses. There were some outdoor stairs that went below the house to a laundry room with a washer and dryer.

During our entire stay, there was only one bolt of lightning, and it was a doosie. We had come back from the beach and had the kids in the tub, and Pam was downstairs at the washer. It was a huge lightning strike, and did significant damage all over the valley, but in our case, a ball of lightning came in the window of the bathroom where the kids were in the tub and rolled around the toilet and then disappeared. It was so loud that our hearing was impaired for a while.

I started yelling for Pam, and she came around the corner looking dazed, and her hair was all frizzled out, with pieces of plastic stuck in her hair, and black smudges across her face. I asked if she was okay, and she just nodded. The lightning had vaporized the phone line, and the phone junction box which was right by Pam's head in the laundry room. The only thing left of the wire and junction box were black smudges on the wall. After a while of stunned shaking, it became evident that we all had survived one more strange event. Although this was the only lightning event in Hawaii, it would not be our last encounter with lightning.

There were also daily earthquakes. Mauna Loa was alive and you could feel her pulsing regularly. Sometimes the quakes were so small you could just feel a slight vibration go through the room like a whisper. Other times it was frightening. There was one particular earthquake that was a 5.5. Now that might not seem big, but to a South Carolina boy who was used to the ground being still and solid, it was enormous. You could actually see ripples move through the ground outside, and dislodged boulders above the house which rolled down like a small car.

Each time I tried to stand up, I was thrown to the floor, and I could see the other side of the house moving several feet in a different direction. The glass in the large glass doors that served as one wall of the house, would twist and emit these very high pitched squeals like they were going to shatter any second, and the big cistern outside rocked back and forth sloshing water over the sides. It lasted for what felt like a long few minutes, and the instant it stopped, the radio started playing "I Feel The Earth Move Under My Feet" by Carole King. The inhabitants here were used to this.....we were not!!!

If I had been able to at that moment, I would have put us all on a plane and left. We didn't have enough money to leave, but it put the thought in our heads. This was not going to be our permanent home.

April 29, 2022

I'm realizing that I could spend the rest of this year with tales of Hawaii, but I'm going to leave much of that for the book. There was a lot of fun and wonder, and a lot of hard work and heartache as well. Because of our relationship with Norman, we had great friends and close relationships with older native Hawaiians, but there was still a lot of anger and resentment among many of the younger Hawaiians, and after our study of the real history of Hawaii, I can say I sort of understand their feelings.

Most days for me were spent working in the coffee land, picking coffee, pruning coffee trees, fertilizing, and probably most of all weed eating. Most of the coffee farmers used paraquat or some other herbicide to kill back the jungle so the coffee trees could grow without competition. Jackie was making every effort to not use herbicides.

This was the first place I ever met a Green Machine, which was the forerunner of the modern hand carried weed eater. It was a strap on 2 cycle rotary head heavy string trimmer. I spent more hours using that thing than I care to remember. I started at the top of the 4-acre farm and gradually worked my way down to the bottom, which usually took about a week.

I could only clear weeds certain hours of the day because of the rain, but sometimes it was necessary to work IN the rain. The "weeds" were mostly what we would consider house plants on the mainland: Impatiens, Begonias, Wandering Jew, and many others. If I kept to my schedule, I was always working in knee deep vegetation. If I missed any time at all, the vegetation got deeper, and if I missed much time on the schedule, I had to start with a sickle and hand cut to get down to where I could use the weed eater again.

By the time I left Hawaii, I could actually hear the jungle growing at night. There was also California grass, which in its natural setting would grow a season, seed, and then die back. In Hawaii it would grow a season, and instead of seeding, it would just keep growing, getting longer and longer until it would climb the trees, and then make a mat on top of the trees. A meadow would develop on top of the trees. Sometimes it would be so thick that the kids would cut a hole and go on top of the meadow on top of the trees.

In the hours when we went to the "beach," we would usually go to Captain Cook Bay at the Heiau. Beach is in quotations, because there is very little actual beach on the Big Island, it's mostly volcanic rock right down to the coast, so we usually said, "Going to the coast, not going to the beach." There were small packets of sand that you could find if you knew where to look. A Heiau is a large stone platform that is a sacred place to the Hawaiians where ritual and sacrifice was made.

There was also another "beach" we frequented that was definitely not a tourist spot, called Keei Beach. It was reached by driving a mile or so across a lava field on what should be called a 4-wheel drive road, although we drove the VW bus across it frequently to get to the beach. At the coast the road went through a small Filipino village where they often had chicken fights in the middle of the road. On those days, there would be a large Samoan man with a radio at the edge of the village who would stop the bus while the chicken fight was going on, and wave us on when there was a break.

The First 60 Days

I just remember him being so large that his hand pretty much covered the driver's side windshield. When he motioned us to proceed, we would slowly go through the village to the other side where there was a tiny little cove of sand and protected tidal pools that were safe for the kids to swim in.

In this village there was a healing woman named Aunty Margaret Machado who had a small healing practice there. There were a few small cabins that people would come and stay in while being treated by Aunty Margaret. We saw her often and talked with her. She seemed interested in our little family and watched us on the beach. Later on we would discover that she was quite famous, and a powerful spiritual leader in the Hawaiian community. Shortly before we left the island, she asked us to play music for her 80th birthday. That was a humbling and amazing experience. There were Hawaiians there from all over the islands, and we were the only white people there to play for Aunty Margaret. She gave us a special blessing after we played, and I think she knew our time in Hawaii was about to end.

We were getting thinner because we weren't eating enough. We were feeding the children as much as we could, and sometimes that meant that we weren't eating. One night Pam went out of the tent to pee, and Pele appeared to her and told her that it was time for us to leave, or we would die here. Pam asked Pele that if the vision was real, to give her a sign. On the beach the next day all of the rocks were black, as usual, except for one white one. When Pam picked up that stone, she cried and looked at me and said, "We have to leave, and soon." We took it into meditation, and talked, and cried together, and talked with the children, and finally came to the decision to leave. We didn't know how we would do it because we had no money and there seemed to be no way out. But as always in our lives, miracles happen.

April 30, 2022

Each day for more than 30 years, our day began with a short reading from *The Daily Word* from Unity Publications, and a simple daily lesson from *The Course In Miracles*. Today's reading from *The Daily Word* is "Let Go, Let God," and the affirmations from The Course are "I rest in God. I am as God created me." These are especially meaningful today because yesterday was the most difficult and emotionally painful since her transition. I guess it was some energetic convergence, the new moon, and the solar eclipse, or something, but whatever it was it hit us all exceptionally hard. Yesterday was a day of sobbing and ground hugging and asking for guidance. I felt more broken than I have ever felt in my life, and it frightened me. This morning seems to be starting out a little better. At least I can take a breath today.

The Escape:

We spent a night in the stars at a friend's shelter high up on Mauna Loa. Way high. Up there, the ground was all volcanic dust in a rainbow of colors. Any small rocks were so full of air holes and light that you could crush them with your hands. There were some fumaroles, or holes where a sulphury smell and warm air came out, like the mountain breathing.

The shelter was nothing more than some boards tacked together with a tin roof. Just one small room like a garden shed. The shelter didn't matter, because it was the mountain and the sky that were the real show. It was cold, and the air was thin, and the stars and sky show were something that we had never been that close to.

The stars and planets were so big and close that it felt like we could touch them. There was no moon, so the stars were especially bright, and the sky was especially black. That blackness is darker than any other black color on earth. This is where the final decision to leave came. A night of soul searching, crying, and family talk.

What really clinched it was our son Josh. He said he just wanted to go see his grandparents. He told us that he felt he had missed a lot of time with them and didn't want to miss any more. The message from Pele, and the message from the heart of a child. We were leaving, whatever that meant. As we went back to our campsite, we began to sell everything that we had. We had a storage room, paid for by some growers who were willing to pay for a storage rental spot if we would sign our name to the rental agreement, and they could also store some pot there. That way if it was busted, it would be us that would be responsible, not the growers. Nice, right? I was beginning to not have good feelings toward the Hippie Mafia, and it seemed like the dream of the age of Aquarius was fading away.

We set up in the Co-op parking lot with all our belongings, and a sign saying we were selling everything. Most everything sold quickly, and we were accumulating our escape fund. Pam was calling the airlines daily looking for a flight. It had to be straight through, with no layovers, and it had to be six one-way tickets.

This turned out to be much, much harder than we thought. It was December, and six one-way tickets were very difficult to find. We were trying to get to Columbia where our family lived, and we hoped/knew that they would help us. Every day the airline told Pam that there was no such

The First 60 Days

flight, and besides, we still didn't have enough money for tickets anyway.

We both took jobs day and night manicuring pot buds. Manicuring bud was a tedious, but satisfying job, even if it didn't pay particularly well. A good manicuring job could mean a substantial difference in the value of the final product.

We were saving everything, and it still wasn't enough. I called friends on the mainland looking for loans....nope. Pam kept calling, and finally one day the airline person said, "Wait a minute. I've never seen this flight before. I have six tickets with stops in LA, Chicago and final destination of Charlotte, NC." It wasn't Columbia, but it was close enough. We had a great friend in Charlotte who would pick us up at the airport. After that, we weren't sure how we would get the last 100 miles, but it was close enough.

That same day, a woman asked to buy our tent, as well as our bus, and we could drop them off at her house on the way to the airport. At that point we really would be homeless. Even with everything gone, we were still several hundred dollars short of the plane tickets. Pam was basically begging our grower friends to loan us the rest of the money. She said she would do anything short of a blow job to secure a loan. Finally, he said he would loan us the money if we would get our parents to repay the loan as soon as we got to Columbia, and he wanted to drive us to the airport.

The day came, and we still had more stuff than we thought. My carpentry and mechanic tools, her cast iron pots and pans, and the ever-present guitar. The day came, and we set off around the mountain in the jeep.

After only a few miles, the jeep broke down. Pam ran to a small Japanese store and called the airlines to see if we could get another flight, and the ticket agent just laughed and said if we didn't get this flight, there was not another chance. Meanwhile, I was frantically working on the jeep. It was a broken water pump, and the closest parts place was miles away.

As always, right at that moment, another friend came driving by, and after a quick explanation, agreed to go get the part. He did, I fixed the jeep, and we were on our way again. The rest of the trip over the mountain to Hilo was quiet and uneventful.

We arrived at the airport shortly before boarding time, and of course the agents wanted to open and inspect every bag and box. While they were doing that, I ran to the restroom and took off my greasy clothes from working on the jeep, threw them in the trash, washed up, and put on fresh clothes. When I got back out, everyone was already boarded, and I had to run on the field to be the last person boarding.

The plane took off, and we were on our way. Pam and me, the four children, and not even a dime to make a phone call. As we left, Kilauea woke up after a 20 year quiet, and has been active off and on ever since. Pele never lies. This was the red eye flight, and it was a long dark night of uncertainty, and yet we were somehow comforted by being together and alive.

April 30, 2022

I'm going to do something I haven't done before. I'm making a second post today. A dear friend and spirit daughter Carol Joy, came from Boston a few weeks ago to give me and my family healing treatments. She is, I think, the youngest advanced Rolfer in the United States, and an amazing energy worker of unparalleled skill and accomplishment. She was here for three days, and gifted sessions to my whole family.

I am beyond grateful, and the shift in our moods and energy was amazing. While she was here, she stayed down at Heartspace, our teaching center, where we taught, and Pam had her healing room.

At some point, Carol Joy wondered what the last music was that Pam was playing on the sound system in her healing room, so she turned it on. It was *Inside Job*, the last recording that Pam and I made. It was so powerful that she just let it play on repeat all day while she was doing the sessions. It was emotional and beautiful to hear her voice while receiving the work. At some point in my session, I heard myself say, "Damn, this is really good, and we did it!!"

Carol Joy said that after she turned the music off at night, sometimes it would come on by itself, and the volume would change. She let it go on, and her husband told her to close the door to the bedroom because he felt Pam was continuing to work in her room. This has happened several times since Carol Joy left.

Carol Joy told me that Pam was continuing her work and she told her to tell us that any time we felt we needed help, to come lay down on the table and ask, and Pam would come and give us a treatment. I have had a great resistance to spending much time at Heartspace, it's just too painful, but after yesterday's grief session I decided it's time.

I prepared myself and went down to the Center. After spending some time looking around at all her "tools," and feeling her presence in the room, I lay down on her table and asked for healing of my heart and emotional body. I started the music, closed my eyes, and waited.

The very first notes caused me to begin to cry heavily and call out loud. Almost immediately, I felt the warmth of her hands on my head and eyes and began to hear her voice telling me to breathe and sink into the table. In the course of the session, she kept telling me "It's okay to be sad, but don't dwell there." As always, she was saying that everything is perfect, and our Love is still present and as close as always. The parts of us that fell in Love cannot be separated. She told me to have courage, and smile some, because I have much work to do yet.

After the session I felt emotionally drained, but much lighter and somewhat better. As I walked outside of the Center, the sky was bright, the breeze in the trees and the sounds of all the birds talking gave me hope.

I turned on my phone and recorded the sounds. If I can figure out how to do it, I will post that recording here. Thank all of you for hanging on out there through these posts and my public grief process. I know our story has much hardship and apparent sadness, but it does get better I promise, and I know I will get better also.

To all of my friends and family who are going through this process of loss of a loved one now, I hope this will bring some comfort in knowing that we are all in this adventure together, and for that I am thankful. Love does win out, even through death.

May 1, 2022

We had made it onto the flight and settled in for the first leg of the flight, the 6 hours to LA.

Night came on quickly since this was the red-eye flight. It didn't take long for the children to fall asleep, and the cabin lights in the plane dimmed and the other passengers began to move into their own methods of nighttime travel. Some would read, some would go to sleep immediately, some would begin hushed conversations, and some, like us, were so wired up with adrenaline and excitement, that we just talked and walked Willie up and down the aisle.

As the night went on, and more and more reading lights went out, things quieted down. Pam noticed this older man with what were obviously his two adult children. They were so tender with each other, and physically loving. After a while, the two children, who were visibly exhausted, fell asleep in the seats. The father gently covered them up with blankets and just sat there looking lovingly at their sleeping forms.

As Pam was walking by with Willie in her arms, trying to get him to go to sleep, she stopped and spoke to the man. She told him that she had been watching the way he was with his children and was in admiration that he could show so much tenderness and love to his adult children, and that she wanted that kind of relationship with our children as we all aged.

They began a conversation and we found out that he was some form of American diplomat, and his children were on their way back from China, which at that time was still not very open. He spoke of his relief that they were safe, and they were on their way home to Washington, DC. After some time in the conversation, he looked deeply into Pam's eyes and said, "I know you and your story. You packed up and went to Hawaii thinking that it would be paradise, found out that it wasn't what you thought, and now you are financially broken and on your way home to your parents. Right?"

With tears in her eyes, Pam asked him how he knew that, and he said he had seen it more times than we could imagine. He told us it was okay to reach for unachievable dreams, and not to despair, that it would be alright. He said to always keep reaching further and not to be afraid. We talked on and off through the night without sleep.

When we landed in LA, we only had a very short time before the next leg took off for Chicago, and we had to run, with sleeping children through the LA airport a long, long way to the next gate. Fortunately, a couple of flight attendants recognized our situation and helped carry the sleeping children and rush us on to get on board just in time. And there was the same man and his children in the seats right across from us. It was sometime around midnight or so, and we weren't sleeping, and neither was he, so the conversation continued and helped keep the darkness away. He spoke of many things like opening up dialog with other countries, and travel to exotic places, and so much more.

He listened intently to our story, and as we landed in Chicago to change planes again, the same thing occurred. We had to run between gates, and were helped by airline attendants, to arrive on the next flight, and here was the same family in the seats across from us on the way to Charlotte. The conversation continued non-stop.

At some point between Chicago and Charlotte, and probably 4 or 5 in the morning, he took Pam's hand and placed an envelope in it. He looked at her with this deep loving look and said, "My wife died this year, and I was wondering what I was going to do for her Christmas gift, and I have found the answer."

He told us not to open the envelope until later. Inside the envelope was $50 and his card with a note telling us if we ever needed anything to call him in Washington. The name on the card was Joseph Kennedy. We tried and tried calling his number after we got home but were never able to find him or contact him again. Fifty dollars was a huge amount of money for us back then.

As we approached Charlotte, daylight was also beginning to break. Just as it was getting light enough outside to see, the pilot came on and said, "Welcome to Charlotte, North Carolina, it's 22 degrees and sleeting, and we'll have you at the gate in about thirty minutes." What??? 22 degrees and sleeting?? We were wearing short sleeve shirts, with flip-flops, and no longer even owned a jacket.

As the plane dropped below the low hanging clouds, and the ground came into view, it was a welcome, familiar sight. The ground looked familiar, the streams and ponds were kind of tomato soup colored with the red clay and the precipitation. It was wet and comforting, but 22 degrees and sleeting. Obviously, we hadn't thought this through.

I'm sure we were a sight. My beard was waist length, as well as my hair. All of the children had long white hair, and Pam had her famous long curly hair. We were all very tan, and very skinny, with our Hawaiian shirts and flip-flops de-planing in the cold air of North Carolina. I could tell we looked weird, because the ocean of people in the airport just parted like the Red Sea, parents grabbed their children, and everyone looked at us with horrified eyes and spoke in hushed tones.

Willie, who had never even seen his breath, was fascinated by the smoke coming out of his mouth. He asked what that was, and we told him it was "cold." He started puffing like a little train around the airport chanting, "Cold, cold, cold." Then we found out that none of our belongings had made it to Charlotte. But just at that moment, our friend Lee pulled up in front in her VW bus, and with intense hugging we got into the bus and felt the heat and went to her house.

She was kind of a thrift store junky and had more clothes than you could imagine. She just bought them because they were a good deal. In short order she had us all outfitted with warm clothes, coats, and most of all some warm food and a place to immediately fall asleep and rest.

Later she drove us to Columbia and dropped us off at my parents' house, who had no idea we were coming. It was December 21st or 22nd, but it was the winter solstice, and near Christmas. We rang the doorbell, and started singing "You Are My Sunshine," which was my mother's favorite song. The door opened, and there was shock and joy and tears on their faces. We had come home, and at that moment, that's all that mattered.

May 2, 2022

There has never been a Christmas more wonderful than the Christmas of 1982. We didn't know what we were doing, we didn't know the next step, we had no plan anymore, but we had family and we were Loved. We felt safe. My parents were so wonderful and understanding and welcomed us in with Love and no hesitation.

There was the evening when a large number of the McMahon Clan came by Christmas Caroling. There was much excitement about our survival and return. My parents had a large motor home that they would travel in, and it was parked in the driveway in suburban Columbia, SC. It was understood that we could stay there for a limited time. It was an absolute luxury compared to our tent life. We had a kitchen, and a bathroom, and living space for all of us that was warm and private. There was even a TV, which we were not accustomed to.

Pam and I were still very angry with what we saw as the collapse of the hippie dream of Love, sharing, and the age of Aquarius. What we were seeing was the dawn of the hippie capitalist drug business and it wasn't pleasant. I didn't want to talk to any of our old friends, or anybody for that matter. I just wanted to withdraw and become "normal."

After the initial couple of days, my father wanted to have "the talk." The talk consisted of a certain level of scolding and lecturing about responsibility, regular work, diet, and our lifestyle. He said I needed to get a haircut, get cleaned up, get some decent clothes, stop smoking weed, get a job, and "settle down." I was so despondent, and grateful for their hospitality and generosity, that I agreed. I shaved my waist length beard, braided my waist length hair, and cut it off.

I presented the braid to my father for a Christmas present. My mother had that braid put in a glass front shadow box, which hung on the wall of their living room until she died, and my father left that house. I tried, I really tried to become "normal." My heart was breaking inside with what I felt like was my complete failure as a father, a provider, and protector.

I got nice clothes, and I applied to a large number of job listings, but was rejected by all of them. As New Year's closed in, Pam and I were getting antsy. Living with my parents was getting to be a strain for them and for us, but we didn't know what to do. I had told my mother that if any of my friends called, please tell them that I wasn't there, and didn't want to talk to anyone.

Of course, the phone rang one morning, and she said, "Oh, he's right here," and handed me the phone. It was some friends who thought we were still in Hawaii and were looking for a way to contact us. When I answered the phone, they were excited and went on about this place where they were living and they thought about us every day because it was exactly the kind of land and community we had always described as the perfect environment. They were going to have a New Year's Eve celebration and said we just had to come.

I told them we had no money and were living in my parents' motor home and couldn't even afford the gas to drive there. They said they had a friend in Columbia who wanted to come up for the party and would pay for the gas if we could just drive up there. I asked my father if we could drive up, and I guess he wanted a break as well, so he agreed. So, on New Year's eve of 1982 we picked up their friend, gassed up and drove to North Carolina for a party. We arrived just before midnight, but were so tired, we parked the motor home, and went to bed.

On January 1, 1983 we woke up to the most beautiful place in the world. The sky was that famous Carolina Blue, the fields were green, the air was sweet and fresh, the rolling hills were covered in hardwood trees, and all of a sudden, life force seemed to stream back into us, and we felt a renewed sense of vitality and hope. This, finally, was paradise! This was Green Creek.

May 3, 2022

The entry into Green Creek was like wandering into wonderland, and our entry into this new life was again magical and also bumpy. That first morning was spectacular. Even though it was the first of January, the temperature was amazingly warm. Not Hawaii warm, but not freezing cold either. We were comfortable without jackets.

Most of our friends from the household were late arising, and hung over, but in our motor home, we could make coffee, and have breakfast and just wander around the fields and down to the small stream, and even venture a short distance into the forest. I had the boys with me, and we were just exploring. I just remember thinking to myself that this is a really beautiful, peaceful place and maybe, just maybe we could find a spot here.

When our friends woke up and found us, they were really excited by our presence and couldn't wait to tell us the story of this community and land. It seems there were two elderly women from Michigan who had similar ideas about the back to the land movement and came here and bought land with the idea of selling small parcels to similarly minded people and living simply and gardening organically.

They were thinking older people would retire here. They put covenants on the land, like no chemical fertilizers, no herbicides, power lines would be underground, parcels could be no smaller than five acres, mobile homes only allowed for the period while you built a house, and those kinds of restrictions.

The First 60 Days

Ms. Zouleck owned the land on the side of the road where we had landed, and Ms. Mullins owned the land on the other side. They both had their quirks but were genuinely nice people. I think Ms. Mullins would allow parcels as small as one acre. It didn't really matter, because only a few older couples came. Most of the families that showed up were young families looking to follow those guidelines and rear their children in a safe, clean environment.

In the early days, Ms. Zouleck had some parcels already surveyed out, but she would also let you just find your spot, survey it, and purchase it. She would owner finance with 10% down and 10% interest, and even with that she was flexible. It was amazing. Of course, we had no down payment, no job, just the thought that this might work for us somehow.

Our parents had already told us that if we would settle down somewhere, they would help us with a down payment. So, we went to meet with Ms. Zouleck to talk about some arrangement to settle here. Our requirements were that we would need a place with at least some kind of house already there, and it had to have access to some kind of water, like stream frontage.

She told us of a place that the first owners had started, and she thought there was a house, but they had moved away 7 years prior and it may be for sale. She told us the general directions to find it, and my friend and I set off to check it out. It was difficult to find, because the road/driveway down to it was about 1/4 mile long, and in very poor condition. In some parts there were small pine trees growing in the middle of the road. It took a while to find the house because it was so overgrown with small pines, vines, and blackberry bushes and was built into the side of the hill. The vines and brush grew right up on top of the roof which you could just walk up on because of being built into the hill.

We sort of chopped our way up to the front door, and I could peek inside. The floor in the front part of the house was oak flooring, and the house was small and in somewhat poor condition from being vacant, but I thought this just might work, so I went back and got Pam and the kids to come check it out. There was some mild enthusiasm on Pam's part, and the kids just explored. We thought that this place was in just about the same condition as ourselves, but it COULD work, maybe.

We were able to get in touch with the "agent" for the house, who was a strange, quirky individual who rode a bicycle and I guess did some kind of maintenance? to the property. He told us that the owner now did not want to sell but would be open to renting it. After some talk, we decided to try it out.

There were some issues inside the house, and it would need repainting inside. Actually, someone had built a fire on the concrete floor in the back part of the house and there was smoke damage. He said to give him some time and he would paint it and then we could move in. We agreed and went back to the motor home.

We didn't realize when we went there that the couple who had invited us there had serious alcohol abuse issues, and in truth, they were well on their way to divorce. It wasn't a pleasant place to stay, and we made plans to leave for Columbia to get ready to move into the little house. Then the winter storm hit.

Carolina weather is fickle. It can be very pleasant one day, and overnight can turn into a blizzard. Snow, sleet, and ice. It's lovely, but not comfortable in a motor home. Loss of electrical power is common. We couldn't leave because the roads were closed. With the alcohol abuse, it became increasingly uncomfortable, and Pam and I began to get physically ill.

Our stay with our friends rapidly deteriorated with the end result being that both Pam and I came down with pneumonia and were deathly ill. We managed to leave as soon as the roads were passable, and went to my parents again, and Pam's mother took her to the doctor and got antibiotics to treat the pneumonia, and my parents took me to my old family doctor for the same treatment. I am so thankful for family. We were really sick and without their help, I'm sure we would have died then.

It took some time to recover, and I kept calling about the house and was told he was painting, and it was not ready. Finally, by March, I called and told him that we were coming, and we would just finish the painting ourselves. We were physically shaky but needed to get on with our lives.

We took the motor home and parked outside the house and lived in it for a week while we finished the painting and got the water working, and the electricity on, and then we moved inside. There was no furniture other than a king size bed in one room, and a funky refrigerator that worked, an electric stove with two working burners and a working oven, but that was it.

We had no furniture, so I found some old cushions out in a shed, and Pam covered them with some fabric, and I made a low table out of scrap wood. We called it eating Japanese style by sitting on the cushions on the floor around the scrap wood table that was our family dining area. I made beds for the two older boys out of foot lockers that I got in Columbia for what clothes and belongings we had.

Oh, I failed to mention that a few days after we got back from Hawaii, the airline called and said our bags had arrived in Charlotte, and our friend Mark Johnson drove us up to retrieve them. That contained my carpentry and mechanics tools, Pam's sewing machine and kitchen gear, and of course the guitar. So, we had those things that enabled me to make repairs and work on the house, and Pam to make covers for the cushions.

After a week, my father wanted the motor home back, so here we were, 15 or 20 miles from any town, no car, no phone, no work, but still together and in a house. There were some obstacles to overcome, and we didn't know it, but we were in what would become our home for the next 40 years. The eagle had landed.

May 5, 2022

Our first few months in Green Creek were pretty tough, even though it was beautiful.

After the return of the motor home to my father, we had no transportation, and we lived at least 15 or 20 miles from the nearest town. I immediately began looking for some kind of employment. That was fruitless to say the least. Our county at that time only had 14,000 residents in the entire county, and that included the three little villages. Our road, which was only 2 miles long end to end, was a small dirt road with 2 tire tracks, and a grass strip in the middle. Our quarter mile driveway was off this road, just about in the middle of those 2 miles.

When we moved into the house, the area around the house was completely overgrown with blackberry vines, small pine trees, and broom sedge. The first day, I remember taking my pocket knife and cutting a small square of clear ground, large enough for a picnic blanket, and we had our first meal on that blanket. All of the area that had once been cleared land was covered thickly in that same vegetation.

A lot of the area was now pine thicket where the young pines were so thick it was impossible to walk through, kind of like a wall of 8 to 10 foot tall trees. I thought it was a good idea to teach my children early how to use hatchets, machetes, and a good sharp knife. They also were taught fire building skills.

This meant they had a healthy respect for sharp tools, and did not play with fire, but used both respectfully and skillfully. So, I gave each of them a hatchet or machete, and told them to go through the pine thickets, and remove all limbs that were low enough for them to reach. It gave them something to do and made it possible for an adult to move into the thickets. They made trails and forts and stayed busy for quite some time.

The very first job I took was as a substitute teacher at the local high school. That was a bizarre experience. Since I had no vehicle, I would walk to the top of our driveway, and catch the school bus with the kids. If that wasn't weird enough, the best clothes I had were Guatemalan hand woven shirts that we had purchased from our friends in Hawaii that were refugees from the war in Guatemala. I also carried a "purse," or hand-woven Guatemalan bag like most of the hippies in Hawaii. I looked like a freak alien to these farm kids and was a hit at the high school.

When I first walked into the office, the assistant principle looked and me and said, "So this is what we're feeding them today....Good luck." The kids in the class were pretty unruly, and weren't really interested in the course work, so they began to ask me questions about where I came from and why I looked like I did.

I began answering questions as best I could without talking about drug use, and we actually ended up having a good time. I got to know quite a few of them well enough to call them friends. But it was obvious that substitute teaching was not going to work.

Through a contact in Columbia, I heard of a construction job at a house renovation site in a transitioning neighborhood. There were still a lot of alcoholics, crack heads, and drug dealers in that neighborhood, but it was beginning to be fashionable to get inexpensive houses there, and renovate them as an investment.

The First 60 Days

I took the job, which meant that I would hitchhike from our house to the bus station in Spartanburg; about 20 miles away, take the Trailways bus to Columbia, and walk the couple of miles from the bus station in Columbia to the job site.

In the beginning, I would stay for a week, sleeping in my sleeping bag on the job site, and working as many hours a day as I could stand. I was doing the job alone except when I would hire a couple of the local guys to help with anything that was too large for me to move on my own.

The condition of the house was pretty bad when I started. There had been a crew that hung the drywall, and they did a terrible job, and it was left completely unfinished. The owner had fired them and the previous renovation crew, which is how I got the job. It was a mess, but I knew how to fix it, and the owner liked my work, so I settled in for what would be a few months of steady work, but it meant that each week, I would do the hitchhike, bus trip there, and back, on the weekend, to deliver the week's wages to Pam and the boys.

In the meantime, Pam had connected with some of the other mothers in the neighborhood, and was able to "car pool," even though we had no car, with these other mothers once a week to the local grocery store, and laundromat. Believe it or not, there was some stability in this routine.

This went on for a couple of months, and then my father, who was the head of the local postal workers credit union, came across a repossessed 1972 Buick, which he purchased for us for very little. This was miraculous!! It meant that Pam would have a vehicle to move the kids around, and fully participate in the "car pool," and even be able to take the kids to the local swimming pool in town. The boys were beginning to make friends and settle in. It also meant that Pam could drive me to the bus station and pick me up as well.

With some money coming in, we had gotten a phone. In those days, we could call our local friends and neighbors with just the last 4 digits of our phone number. It still meant that I stayed on the job site and walked back and forth from the bus station in Columbia, so it wasn't easy, but it was better than the hitchhiking.

Pam and I had never spent a night apart until I was doing this job, and a new dynamic was developing. She was working out a way of organizing our lives without me in it during the week, and in some ways, when I would come home for the weekend, it would disrupt the new flow. This began to create some personal and marital issues between us, and I was hoping for some way to get work closer to home.

Instead, I finished the job in Columbia, and the next job I could find was working finish construction with a Vietnam vet friend in Atlanta. This meant staying on the job for 2 weeks or more at a time. In addition, this friend had a cocaine issue, and we would often work 16 or 20 hour days. Sometimes we would just work straight through without sleep.

I was not doing cocaine, and this pace became unworkable for me, and the separation was putting added strain on our relationship, so I quit and came home. Luckily, a couple in the neighborhood who were building a house, hired me to finish it. This was absolutely fantastic. It was only a mile away down the dirt road, and it meant I could leave my tools there, and live at home.

What a blessing to be able to be with Pam and the children full time again, and close enough so that often Pam would bring me lunch and we could have more time together. We were starting to make the adjustment to my full-time participation in the family again.

When that job was finished, I did one more house building project, but then I wanted to get out of the construction business, because I still had all my fingers, and liked playing guitar too much. At this point, a lady friend of Pam's came by who was a basic skills teacher and was leaving her job and wondered if I might not be interested.

It was part time teaching basic reading skills to local residents, and the classes were at night in the local school just at the end of our road. I enthusiastically accepted this offer and was hired right away.

Basic reading skills. When I took this job, the illiteracy rate in our county was about 65% functionally illiterate. Which meant I was teaching adults to read for the first time. Many needed to learn to read for a promotion in their jobs, and some wanted to be able to read the Bible, and many other reasons, but it was fulfilling and rewarding to watch the spark of reading begin in these people.

My oldest student was in her 80's, and the light in her eyes when she actually began to read for the first time was really something to behold. It made me so thankful for my own education, and that my children all loved reading.

I kept doing that job for 5 years, gradually getting more classes and started to teach adult high school and GED preparation, and eventually I started teaching computer literacy classes. The computer literacy classes are how I finally began to find my place as an IT consultant to local governments. I continue in that role today.

In the course of teaching basic reading, and helping students get a high school diploma or GED, I ended up teaching somebody in almost every family in the county, and I got to know a lot of them well.

At the same time, Pam was having issues of her own. She was not well. She was thin, and getting thinner. She felt she had parasites from living in the tropics for ten years. She was tested for pin worms, and tapeworms, which was all they knew how to test for out here, but she felt that it was more than that. This is when Chief Two Trees came into our lives, and I will continue with that next time.

May 6, 2022

It's very early morning here in Green Creek, and there is a welcome, gentle rain falling as occasional thunder rolls in the darkness outside. My little friend Kiki and I sit here by the lamplight while I have my morning lemon water and begin to write more.

I was working hard and Pam was working harder I think. Where we had shared a lot of the child care duties before, now this was largely left to her, along with the Home Making. She was doing a heroic job with the assets she had to work with, but it was really difficult, and her health was suffering. Each day she was getting thinner and had less energy.

We reached a point where she would get up in the morning, make breakfast for the children and then have to go back to bed again. Sometime later, she was so exhausted, she couldn't get up to make breakfast, so I began to do that, and take her meals to her in bed.

We began to think she had some terrible disease and might be dying. She had gotten so ill that she was no longer even able to smoke her precious weed. We didn't have much faith in the medical community and the few tests that she got gave no definitive results, and she was resigning herself to an early passing.

One of the first things I had done after we moved in was to find the garden space, and plant vegetables and some herbs. For some reason I had planted a lot of parsley. One day, while I was at work, a neighbor came and said that he heard we might have some parsley, and wondered if he could get some from us. Pam told him that we had quite a bit in the garden, and he was welcome to whatever he needed, but she wondered why he needed it.

He said that he had a large kidney stone, and was going to have to have surgery, and that he had gone to this Cherokee Medicine Man named Chief Two Trees who told him that if he would drink this parsley tea in quantity, that he could reduce the size of the stone, so that it could pass. Pam was intrigued and asked about the Chief. He told her how she could find him in Old Fort, which was about an hour away.

She was in no condition to drive, but a couple of the local neighbors offered to take her up there. I'm telling you that the generosity and closeness of our neighbors then was truly something to be cherished.

So, one day they carried her up to see the Chief. There was no process of making appointments or check in or anything like that, if you needed the Chief, you just showed up. If you look up Chief Two Trees on the internet, there will be many stories that portray him as a charlatan or fake. We were there, and our experience with the Chief was anything but fake, it was life altering, lifesaving, and changed the course of the rest of our lives.

It was counter intuitive though. He lived in what could be called a shack with a front porch and a somewhat barren yard with broken trucks and vehicles, some of which had mangy dogs living underneath them. It was the kind of place that could easily make you fearful of some kind of horrible deep south redneck experience. In the back was a round hut like building that could seat maybe 15 or 20 people around the wall, and in the center was a massage table. This was his teaching and healing center.

When you came in, you quietly took one of the seats around the wall, and waited. The Chief was not a particularly large man, but his presence was huge. He slowly walked around the building smoking these small cigars and blowing smoke near the participants. He circled the group several times like this, and then stopped in front of Pam and said, "Lady, I don't know who you are, or where you've been, but you have the worst case of parasites in anyone that I have seen, who is still standing."

Pam said that in her head she heard, "Hallelujah, I have found my healer!!" He told her that she might be able to save herself if she would do exactly what he said, and that it might take 18 months to get her back to full health, and that if she was not willing to do that, that she should leave. She agreed, and that began a close, intimate relationship that lasted until the Chief died in 1995.

In his healing center, as he worked with different people, he had an assistant who would follow him, and as he spoke a litany of herbal compounds and vitamins and supplements, they would be writing it down. Everything was out in the open in front of all the people there. Your turn would come, and you would go to the table and receive a chiropractic adjustment while he "smoked" you, and began the recitation of directions for your treatment regimen. There was no privacy.

He told Pam that there was no need for supplements for her because everything she was eating, or supplements that she was taking, were being consumed by the parasites in her body. He said the first thing to do was to kill the parasites and then begin rebuilding her body. He gave her a prescription for about $100 dollars' worth of compounds from a local health food store, and told her to begin and come back in a week.

She didn't have the money for the compounds, but one of the ladies with her told her she could charge them on her credit card and Pam could pay her back later. There were a lot of pills to take daily, and she was to blend up 1 can of asparagus, with a whole head of garlic, and a large portion of cayenne pepper, and eat that daily, with not much else. She was committed, and gagged this mixture down every day, along with the handful of pills, and a lot of water. I can't remember how long this went on, but maybe two weeks.

Then it happened. It was a full moon, and all of a sudden Pam spiked a high fever, like really high. She became delirious and started thrashing around. One of her good friends was a nurse, and was here with us, and we began to bathe her with ice and alcohol to try to get the fever down. It wasn't working. She was now having visions or hallucinations, and the nurse and I were starting to freak out. I finally called the Chief and told him what was happening.

He was quiet for a moment, then said something about the full moon, and this was really good and powerful, and a few other things, and I can't remember the time he said, but something like two and a half hours, and it would all be over. Pam had faith in the Chief and would not allow us to take her to the hospital, and exactly two and a half hours later, the fever broke, she sat up in bed and said, "I feel great!!, and I'm hungry!!" We started feeding her soup, gave great thanks, said prayers, sang healing chants, and then the real healing began.

May 7, 2022

Well, the storms of Friday have past, and that lovely rain that has greened our world has caused an explosion of bird calls, Spring growth and new life.

When Pam had her miracle healing and sat up in bed, she was thin, but hungry and ready to spring into life. The Chief began to rebuild all of her internal systems and organs, one by one over the next six months, and she just got better and better.

Let me say a few more things about the Chief. Money. He never asked for any kind of payment. There was a large mouth gallon jar on a table by the door, with a sign that read, "$10 Suggested Donation." He never checked to see if anyone actually put money in the jar or not. There was absolutely no pressure for any kind of payment.

Of course, everyone who could pay something did put money in the jar. There were quite a few times when we "paid" for Pam's visits with baskets of vegetables from our garden, and he seemed very excited by that, and would turn around and have his wife prepare them and share them with his "patients."

He always had a young wife. He went through a couple while we were with him. It's very hard to be the medicine man's wife. I learned later that it's also very hard to be the medicine woman's husband. Medicine people tend to give themselves away. They never turn anyone away who is genuinely asking for help.

We watched the Chief work continuously all day, and periodically his wife would bring him food or water. Any time we arrived, there would already be people there, whether it was at daylight, or even late into the evening. We were there, in the beginning, usually twice a week, or more frequently, so we got familiar with some of the other "patients."

There was this one older black man who appeared quite frail and had a large number of skin lesions. One day, the Chief admonished him, telling him that he had not been taking the vitamins and supplements that he recommended. He sheepishly told the Chief that he could not afford them.

We watched the Chief pick up the phone and call the health food store that sold his supplements and gave a long list to the lady on the phone. At the end of the conversation, he told her to put it on his tab, and the man would be by later to pick them up. We saw this happen on several occasions.

Other times he might tell the person that if they couldn't afford a particular supplement, he would have them eat bone marrow from a ham bone or other possibilities. His point was that you did what he told you without question.

Pam's health improvement was amazing, and she was becoming so healthy that after six months she felt good enough to start smoking weed again. Her healing progress slowed down, and on one visit the Chief looked intensely at her and asked, "Do you want to tell me what's going on?"

I watched Pam squirm and shrink down and remove her eyes from his gaze and said, "Chief, what do you think about marijuana smoking?" Chief jumped up from his seat and towered over her and began to speak really loudly, almost shouting at her. He got right up in her face, and began with, "I can't believe that you would waste your time with this. After all we have done, and the progress we have made? There is so much that you need to do, and so much healing that you can offer this world, and you choose to do drugs instead? I'll give you 1 week to completely stop this and any other drugs that you are doing, and if you don't come back here next week being 1 week clean, do not ever come here again. Don't call me, and don't contact me in any way. Your life and time may not mean much to you, but my time is too precious to waste on anyone who would choose to waste theirs. Now get out of here!"

We were both crying. There was little conversation on the ride home. She did not smoke anything that day, although she really wanted to. That weekend we were playing for a friend's wedding, and at the reception, of course, we went to the "smoking circle." As the joint came around the circle and reached Pam, she looked at it, and held it for quite some time, then she turned, looked at me, and passed it to me and said, "I'm done." I passed it on without smoking, and that was the end of our 20 year relationship with weed. She never engaged in that activity again for the rest of her life.

She realized that she was an addict. It wasn't easy for her to not smoke, and it took a couple of years before she felt comfortable around other smokers without wanting to smoke. She described her feelings as, "I'm not going to smoke right now. Maybe later, but not right now." This would be her mantra, and she said that in the beginning it was almost every minute that she would have to remind herself. Sometimes she would get very angry and act out, but she continued her abstinence.

She said that she knew she did everything in an addictive way, and the only way to get past the bad addictions was to pick better addictions. She started beading earrings and crystal pendants. They were beautiful and gallery grade pieces. I fixed up a small shed out back that was my workshop as her new healing space where she could go and lock the door and work on beading addictively and be alone.

She became absolutely fanatical about crystals and learned much from the Chief as well as her own research. We would drive up to Spruce Pine to the mineral fairs to get crystals of various kinds. She became good friends with Ted Ledford, who was a rock dealer and had a great selection of raw material.

He had been an old miner in the area and had a dream of getting enough money together to lease the old Crabtree Mine, which had been the Tiffany mine for emeralds, but had been mined out and closed for years. He felt there was still a sweet spot in that mine, and did manage to lease it. We were there the day that he brought out these beautiful clear green emeralds the size of my forearms. Just to stand close and touch these made you feel giddy and lightheaded.

Pam became so involved in making her crystal jewelry, that she went to Arkansas to meet with Ocus and Irene Stanley, who owned the Fisher Mountain mine. At that time, the very best quartz points came from there. This was before the big explosion of interest in crystals. Pam would hand pick all the points she wanted for her jewelry. They gave her the name "High Grade Hannah" because she was so particular about the purity and sharpness of the points. No defects were acceptable.

She used this obsession to assist her in her continuing abstinence, and it worked. Personal power and energetic healing was becoming her new addiction, and she was really good at it. She was finally finding her true place and purpose in the world. The Chief was extremely proud of the medicine woman she was becoming.

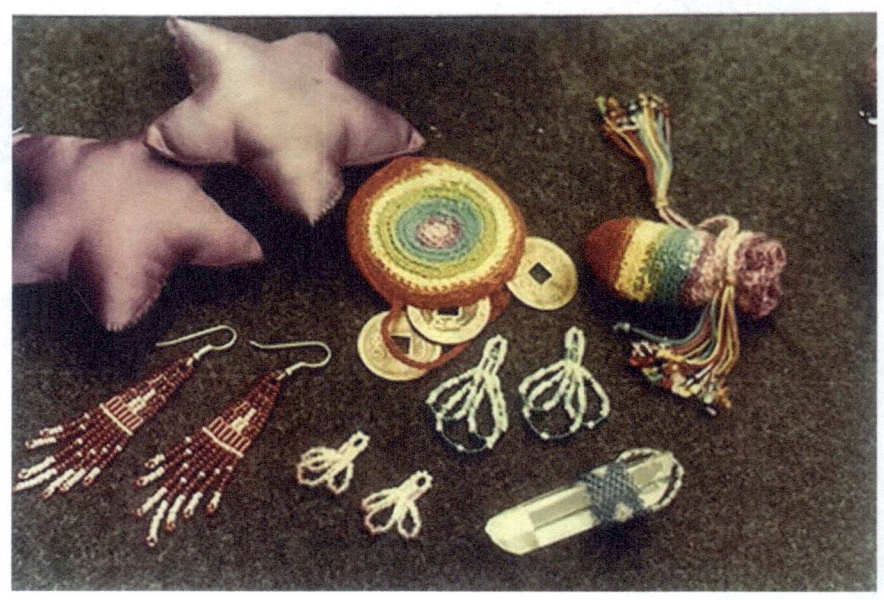

May 8, 2022

We worked closely with the Chief until his death in 1995. I had my own miracle healing with him.

After that day when he scolded her for her pot use, she was diligent in following his instructions, and over the next year she became strong and healthy. He convinced her that her effort to become totally vegetarian was not in her best interests. He would say, "Look at your teeth. You come from a long line of meat eaters. Cultures who are routinely vegetarian have grinding teeth, and meat eaters have sharp canines. You are trying to modify your diet too much in one generation." She didn't like it, but she began to gradually include fish and poultry in her diet. It made a big difference. After she fully recovered, it seemed like it was my turn.

One night around Halloween, a friend had been visiting and when he got ready to leave, his car wouldn't start. After some inspection, in order to keep working on his car, I went in and grabbed a jacket because it was turning cold. It was a jacket I had not put on since the prior year. After I helped him get his car started, I went back in to get Willie ready to go to a Cub Scout meeting.

I noticed a pain in my left elbow and checked it out. It was a small bite like a wasp sting, and there was a red swelling in the area. Pam had been taking Swedish Bitters, which is an herbal compound that we would make each month by soaking these herbs in EverClear alcohol for a period and then straining off the herbs.

Chief told us to put the wet herbs in a cloth and put them in the freezer. If we ever got a bite, or skin rash, or even a bruise, we could use it as a poultice, and it would sooth the area and draw down any swelling. So, I got one of those out and put it on the bite, and took Willie to his meeting. By the time we got back home, my arm was beginning to hurt all the way up to my shoulder, and the area immediately around the bite was getting very hot.

Overnight, I continued to apply the herbal packs, and by morning the pain was substantially reduced, so I got up and went to work and didn't think much about it. Exactly one week later, I became violently ill with fever, vomiting, diarrhea, and intense joint and muscle pain. There were some kinds of viruses going around and I thought I had caught something so I went to bed and tried to eat soup and liquids.

Several days went by and I was getting worse. It felt like someone had beat me with a baseball bat, and I kept complaining that I hurt inside, more so on the left side. Finally, it was Buddy that said, "Pop, isn't that the side where you had that bite last week?" In a flash I realized that the bite was something more than a wasp sting. Also, by that time, the glands on the base of my neck had swollen to the point that they were pushing my head forward, and I was becoming extra sensitive to light. Pam called the Chief, and he said to get me there immediately, that it could be a Brown Recluse spider bite.

I was so sensitive to light that on the ride up to the Chief, I had to have a cloth cover over my eyes. When we got there, I could only walk with assistance. I sat at his table, and he gave me a large glass of what I can only describe as a bitter mud, and told me to drink the entire thing, which I did. He said that within a few minutes we would know if it was indeed a spider bite. Incredibly, within 15 minutes, all of my symptoms were gone, and I felt great.

He said that the good part was that we know what it is, and the bad part is that in 4 hours, the symptoms would all be back, and that I would need to drink this concoction every 4 hours for quite some time. He said that usually this spider bite would cause necrosis of tissue at the site, but because I had used the herbal pack, the venom had gone internal and was attacking my organs. I was literally being dissolved inside.

Over the next 4 hours, sure enough, the symptoms returned with a vengeance, so it was easy to remember to take the remedy frequently, and I began to gradually feel better. About a week or 10 days into the treatment, I was feeling good enough to continue working on a computer program that I was writing for a client when I noticed that I was not thinking clearly.

I couldn't follow the logic of my prior work. The next day, I couldn't read at all. I could make out all the letters on a page, but I couldn't make words. If you asked me a simple question, like what is 4 plus 4, I would start to answer, and in my head, I was scrambling around thinking, "I know the answer to this, but I can't seem to find it." I was getting frantic, like I was looking through a big bookcase for something and being unable to find it. It was extremely frightening.

We called the Chief, and he said that the venom was attacking the base of my brain and prescribed massive doses of PABA. It began to work, and I started to recover. After that the Chief said to me, "I want you to remember that feeling of knowing what you want to say, but not being able to find the answer, and being lost in your head. That is autism, and you will be able to use that feeling to help others later."

It took nearly a year before I felt fully recovered, and during that time I couldn't work, and we were living on credit cards. That was the beginning of a long period of indebtedness. I'm telling you this long story because it will become important later as well.

All of this took place in the mid 1980's. The whole time, Pam was busy learning from the Chief and reading, and going through more education in energy healing, crystal work, meditation, and growing in her own personal healing energy and methods. Pam, from birth, had this ability to say just the right thing at the right time to help people.

We could be in a Walmart checkout line, and the cashier would start crying and telling Pam her most private, painful thoughts, and somehow Pam would be able to help her. It would happen everywhere, and I soon began to accept this as normal. All of the marijuana, alcohol, and drug use was her avoiding her inner guidance to follow her true spiritual calling. She truly was a medicine woman and even she was beginning to realize it.

May 10, 2022

Green Creek was a wonderful place to land. That first year was so hard adjusting to life in this new land, as well as glorious. Having to be separated for work, and becoming part of a different community. Even though it was beautiful, and the neighbors were wonderful and so helpful, there was still that wanderlust and missing the road, and more than anything else, missing the ocean.

For the prior 10 years we had never been very far from the ocean, and it was our rest and rejuvenation place. Our mother. And now we were far from her. The feeling of loss was immense. Often, we would go down to the creek, sit and put our feet in the water and cry. We would remind each other that if worse came to worse, we could always just follow the creek downhill, and eventually we would find our way back to the ocean.

It seems odd now to remember that feeling since we became so comfortable in these welcoming mountains and hills. We had come from the newest land on earth, to some of the oldest. The mountains here are old. The Appalachian Mountains used to be as tall or taller than the Himalayas. Over eons they have been worn down to the heart of the mountains. The gold and precious gems from deep in the earth are on or close to the surface.

She is moist and fertile here. Between each of the rolling, tree-covered hills there is a stream. And mostly the streams are clean and sweet without the fouling of civilization. Sometimes I look from the front door at the soft, brown hills and they seem like breasts. Mother Earth in her worn and loving repose. At rest. It's easy to be grateful here. It appears safe, comfortable, and healing.

At the end of the first year, the owner called and told us that they were thinking of moving back, and we should begin looking for another place. I immediately freaked out, as I was prone to do, and thought that I needed to fix things. We had come to love it here, and I started frantically looking for some other living arrangement. Pam did not. She kept saying that this was our place, and he was not ever going to actually move back, and she continued life as if it was all going to work out just fine.

The second year, he did the same thing, and we each reacted the same way. Then one day, I think actually it was Mother's Day, he called and said, "I'm going to make you an offer that you can't refuse." and proceeded to tell us that he wanted to sell the place to us, and he wanted 10% down, and he would finance it for 10 years, at 10%. We were completely taken off guard, and it took some minutes to realize what he was saying.

We had no idea where we would come up with the down payment, but we said yes, yes, yes. Between Pam's parents, and my parents, they loaned us the down payment. We didn't believe in land ownership at that time. From our time with native peoples, we had an understanding that you couldn't OWN the land, you belonged to the land.

When I said this to the lawyer who was completing the sale, he said, "Well, just pretend you own it then." I said, "You mean that all I have to do is sign these papers, and I can pretend that I own this land?" He agreed with that. We signed the papers and became the stewards of 11 1/2 acres of forested land with a creek, garden, deep clean well, and a small house, for $27,000. We finally had an actual home.

We could continue in earnest to care for this land with the knowledge that we were temporary custodians, and we should treat it as a sacred obligation. I think this was 1985. Pam was spending more time beading and working with crystals and ceremonies with many people, with a growing sense of duty to teach and act purposefully in a healing way.

The first Harmonic Convergence happened in August 16-17, 1987. As this time approached, Pam felt it was necessary that we do some kind of ceremony and event to commemorate the momentous occasion. She started planning and coordinating with others to make this our first gathering on our land. She printed flyers and sent postcards and talked to lots of people. I had concerns that she was inviting so many people to our land. I felt protective and was concerned that they would damage our place. She just kept going.

Then as the day arrived, people started appearing. More people started appearing. In all, over 300 people showed up to camp and celebrate. In all the promotion, she had clearly stated that this was to be a "no drugs, no alcohol" event. By then, she was clean, and she was very serious about her ceremonies.

They came from all over the southeast and set up camp. Pam had everything scheduled. There were workshops, Sufi dancers, music and chanting, and community meals. It was amazing. She had a big school bell, which she would ring to call everyone to gather. You could hear that bell for a mile.

The very first thing she did was get them together and make the rules clear about garbage consciousness. There was to be no trash left, and they were responsible for removing all their trash. The land was to be treated with respect, and

NO fires other than the main community fire, and no cutting of trees or brush.

I only had to escort one person away. He was drunk when he got here, and I made sure he left. It was a wonderful weekend, and we met so many people who became life-long friends. We had a sweat lodge for the first time.

I had asked the Chief for permission to do this, and instructions, because I had never done it before. He gave me simple instructions for building the sweat lodge, and when I asked him about starting the fire to heat the stones, he said "All you white people go around trying to start a fire by rubbing sticks together or with flint/steel. Me, I just Flick my Bic."

He laughed and told us to be respectful and careful, and we would be guided if we just asked Spirit what to do. It was truly an amazing gathering, and when it was over, I walked the land to survey the damage. There was no trash, and it was very difficult to tell that 300 people had been camped there. Just the feeling of all those who participated was left in the woods. That was an empowering event, and initiated much, much more.

May 11, 2022

Given all the craziness of the world and political situation I feel like I want to rant!! But I won't out of respect for Pam, and this is in fact HER page, not mine. For the last 50 years, she has been my governor and kept me and my mouth out of conflict, and now that she's not here, I am dangerous and try to be overly cautious in what I write here.

No matter how hard you try to keep your children safe and sheltered, as they grow up they find their way into the world. It wasn't long before they began to discover the mall and a whole other community of kids. At different times, they became mall rats, skateboarders, punk music listeners, screamers, mash pit regulars and other things that were so foreign to Pam and me.

They began to spend more time in town and were exposed to all that goes with that. As they began to discover other children of similar tastes and feelings, they found many of them who were latch key kids, single parent kids, runaway kids, kids from abusive situations, generally disaffected youth, and began to bring them home.

When we were alone with our children they would say with amazement, "There's nobody home at their house, and they don't have much to eat, can we bring them home?" In this way we began to host quite a few young people as extended family. They would often stay with us for quite some time. There were lots of "parties," where there would be alcohol and weed usage, and Pam would take their car keys and not let them leave if they were compromised, so there were a lot of sleepovers.

She discovered early that part of the reason they got so drunk was because they weren't eating well. She began to feed them. You would never guess their surprise reaction to something as simple as spaghetti and Ragu sauce. It made a huge difference in their attitudes, and so gradually introducing better food to them was a project of hers.

Frequently I would build a big bonfire, and roast hot dogs and marshmallows. It was amazing how many of them had never done that and were so happy and excited to learn these simple things. We often say that we had 4 sons, but we raised 75 children. We only lost a few, and frequently in the passing years, there would be some who would come back or call on Mother's Day, or Christmas. Most of them would refer to us as Mom and Pop, or Madre and Padre.

I know this may seem odd or dangerous to some, to allow this kind of behavior, but we figured they were going to do it anyway, and at least here we knew they were safe and could be monitored. There was really only one rule in our home. Always tell the truth. No matter how hard, or what you have done, always tell us the truth.

Pam used to remind me frequently, that if you expect them to tell you the truth, you can't freak out when they do. It's our job to just listen, and hopefully offer some helpful advice. After all, we had personal experience with all those drugs, and some level of that lifestyle. We never hid any of our behavior either, and the kids got to see us doing drugs, but more importantly, they got to see us stop using drugs, and so we had credibility.

And I think that pretty much all the time they did tell us the truth, and over time we found a deep level of trust with them and by doing so, we heard so much more than we ever expected. Remember Donald T., don't freak out when they tell you the truth.

A lot of times it was all I could do to not respond by intervening with their parents or families, in ways that would not be helpful. I am so thankful that Pam was in my life and taught me the "gentle way." I had been a soldier, and we dealt with unwanted behavior in a much different way.

It was during this time, that I discovered just how broken I was from my Vietnam experience and began a conscious process of working on my own psychological and spiritual healing journey. Even 15 years after my military experience, I was often having nightmares, and sometimes waking up on the floor, or under the bed.

It is so weird that I assumed that was normal behavior. Sometimes I would wake up from the nightmares, not knowing where I was, and Pam would hold me very tightly, and whisper to me, "You're not there, you are here with me. Look around. Right here, right now everything is alright." She would repeat those words over and over until I could calm down. I hear those words in my mind right now as I write this.

Those words would keep me sane and help me through my fears and worries for the rest of my life. Even now as I hear them in my heart instead of with my ears. I would never physically harm my children or Pam, and whenever we would have a heated argument, or I felt out of control, my method of dealing with it was to remove myself from the situation, to go into the woods, or just away until I could calm down.

After my experiences on my return from Vietnam, I learned to hide everything. I thought that if I just forgot about it, and never told anyone I was a veteran that it would eventually go away. It doesn't. Those feelings of anger, fear, and rage don't just go away, they hide inside and fester like an untended wound. After 10 or 15 years of denial and hiding, something had to give if I was to continue to be a good father and husband. So, I began the real journey of coming home.

May 12, 2022

The last two nights I have actually "slept" in our bed. Since Pam's passing I have not been able to bring myself to sleep in our bedroom. It's not a bad thing, just an emotional thing. So, I've been sleeping on the fold out sofa bed in the TV room. Something about the white noise of the TV can put me to sleep in seconds. I know that's not a long term beneficial way to sleep, plus it's actually much more comfortable in our bed....just lonely.

What I'm going to write about today is personal, and in no way is advice of any kind, it was just my way of processing my way through my Vietnam experience. There will be no gruesome war stories, all of that part will still remain private.

Through the decade and a half of denial, guilt, and shame since my exit from the Army, I had become afraid of actually examining my inner landscape. I kept telling Pam that I felt like I had been wounded in some deep way and had bandaged the wound with a field dressing, and never looked under the bandage.

I was afraid that if I looked, I would realize that the wound had become infected and gangrenous and that if I saw what was under there, that I would possibly die. She kept reassuring me that it was okay, and when I was ready, she would help me unbandage the wound, clean it out, and that it would be the only way for me to move through my fears.

One night, after a lot of hesitation, I agreed to look if she would help me. I got on the bed, and she gently started me breathing and gently massaging me and basically guiding me into a meditative state. So, in my mind I unwrapped the wound, so fearful about what I would find. When I looked, I realized that I had suffered trauma and was emotionally wounded, but instead of a nasty wound, there was a scar. A scar that I could look at and touch and soothe.

Now keep in mind that this is all in my head, I was lucky enough to not have received any serious physical wounds, no purple heart. I had a massive emotional response to finding the scar, and began on phase two of recovery, working my way out of denial. I realized that I had been in denial so long that I didn't even know what was real about my experience, and what had become fantasy in my mind, so I began a process of conscious remembering. Going over every day and every action that I could bring into focus so that I would be fully present with the Truth.

It took several years of this remembering before I was satisfied that I knew what had happened, and then I was really angry. Angry with the situations that I had been put in, angry with the lies that put me there, angry with all the people involved with the lies. Anger is not a good place to be but was a necessary step.

Then, through dialogue with Pam, and much meditation I realized that the only way through the anger was through forgiveness. This was a big step. Forgiveness. What a concept. But I knew that if I was going to move forward, this was the only way, and I began a year's long journey of forgiveness. Forgive all the people that I felt had put me in this place, forgive all those who had lied, forgive all those that would not listen, forgive the lady at the draft office, who was a neighbor, who blankly stared at me when I said that I wanted to appeal my draft and loss of student deferment, forgive my parents for not intervening, and forgive God for allowing war to happen.

In the end, I realized that it was me I needed to forgive. That was the hardest part. When it came down to the Truth, it was me. I was responsible for the decisions that I had made. I was responsible for allowing myself to be manipulated against my own inner knowing, not anyone else. It was me. The next few years were spent in deep reflection and inner work on forgiving myself and restoring my faith and relationship with God, or Great Spirit, or Creator, whatever you want to call that. Eventually I came to resolution and thought that I was whole again, and it felt good. Then came the next phase.

Chief Two Trees had called me to a meeting with some other men from around the country to talk about community, and ecological issues. I was honored to be there. There was a circle of about 20 men, and I was seated with two native men on my left, and a white man on my right. While we were waiting for the meeting to begin, somehow, I was talking to the white man on the right and telling him the story of the Brown Recluse spider bite. I was being descriptive and telling him about the pain and year-long recovery process, when all of a sudden, the Indian man on my left, leaned over to me and said, "Stop whining." I stopped dead still and flushed somewhat, and said, "What did you say?" Again, he said, "Stop whining."

I was offended, and puffed up and said something, and he stopped me and said, "There was something inside of you that you were not able to get out, so the Spider People gifted you with the bite to help you remove it. You should be thanking the Spider People for the gift, and instead you are whining." Then he just turned around and went back to stoically and quietly staring about six feet in front of himself.

I was completely overwhelmed with what he had said. Lights went off in my head. I had never in my life considered looking at this situation from that perspective. I don't remember what the meeting was about because I spent the rest of it in deep personal reflection. What did this mean? How could I look at that terrible experience with gratitude?

Then it started to make sense. Forgiveness was only a step toward gratitude, and if I could find some way to be thankful for the spider bite, it could translate over into all the rest of the painful experiences in my life. This was a completely foreign and new way of thinking for me, but in my heart, I knew he was right.

I began a personal practice of gratitude. The first thought in my mind each day as I woke up was, "I am thankful for this day and that I am awake." The last thought before falling asleep at night would be the same. When I woke up to pee, the same thought would be there. Many, many times during the day, the thought would be there, a reminder to be thankful for all be blessings in my life, even when they seemed like challenges. I became obsessive with gratitude. My entire life began to change. Things that would normally make me angry or frustrated, became new ways to find gratitude. It became my "go to" for dealing with daily issues.

Somewhere during this period, we became friends with two native people, Yolanda was a Mescalero Apache, and Woody was a Lakota Sioux. We became very close and good friends. They were going to sponsor a Pow Wow, and asked if we would sing for it. We had never attended a Pow Wow, but they asked, and we agreed.

In the organizational meetings there was a good bit of resentment that we would be playing at a native Pow Wow, but Woody replied to the complainers that the Circle was not complete until all colors were represented. We were the whiteys. They also asked me to supply my PA system, and run the mixing board.

At the Pow Wow, there were 2 big drums, one Lakota, and one Cherokee. I had never heard anything like this. As the drums and chanting began, it would vibrate your insides. At first, as it continued, it almost became irritating, but then I moved into this trancelike state, and I really began to experience the power of the Drums.

In a Pow Wow, as I learned, the first song is a dedication and consecration of the circle where the dances would occur. There was a big procession of dancers with full regalia, led by the Medicine Man who carried the staff. The whole procession was followed in by some veterans with rifles and in mixed garb of jungle fatigues and feathers and native clothing. They followed behind, firing shots in the air, and protecting the People and the Circle. This was in gratitude to Creator.

When they were preparing for the second dance, Woody came to me and said, "This is the veteran's dance." I said, "Okay, I've got this and I'll get the sound right." Woody said, "No, this is the veteran's dance. This is where we honor the veterans, without whose service, none of this would be possible." I said, "Okay Woody, I've got this." He said, "No, this is the veteran's dance...this means that you must dance." I tried to decline, saying that I didn't know anything about dancing, and I was running the sound. Woody became agitated and said, "NO! This is the veteran's dance, and you must dance."

Reluctantly, I walked out into the circle of men and women veterans, and the drums and chanting started. I began dancing the best I could, trying to follow the rhythmic steps of the others. All of the dancers were also in the circle in full regalia. After several trips around the circle, I was again getting into a trance. Then the dancers started to peel off and form two lines, with a pathway between them. Then the veterans began to dance out of the circle in between the two lines of dancers. As we passed through, each one of them looked us in the eyes and said, "Thank You. Welcome Home." By the second "Thank You," we were all crying, and I became so weak I could hardly stand, and other veterans supported me when I waivered. I will be forever thankful for The People, their honoring, and that ceremony. I was finally home.

May 13, 2022

Sweet, gentle rain this morning. I'm late rising because I actually slept some hours last night. Ah, sweet, dreamless sleep also. I wake up thankful again for all the blessings in my life. Everything in my world now is dreamlike, moving from one task to another always, holding sorrow and gratitude closer than my clothes. As I tell these stories I sometimes wonder, "Was all this real?? Does 76 years of human life condense down into a few tales of struggle and joy? What am I doing?"

I have no Facebook presence other than writing through Pam's page. This whole Facebook journey that I'm on began, in my initial shock, as a simple declaration and explanation of Pam's death so that her friends and loved ones in Facebookland would know of her passing and quell the circulating rumors of how it came about. Now it has taken on a life of its own, and I'm just along for the ride as a storyteller.

I don't know where this is going, but I can see by the wonderful comments and messages I get, that some of these stories are way outside of certain reader's experiences, and others touch and comfort places and feelings in some that are all too familiar and relatable. I continue humbled and thankful in the belief that in the grand scheme of things, that this means something, and is possibly helpful to some.

Money. It is obvious that money, or lack of it, is a common theme in all most of these stories. This was a creation of our own. Pam and I both bought into the thought form that "Money is the root of all Evil." In our early years, both of us were friends with and had exposure to people with vast monetary wealth. In the beginning, the rich and famous lifestyle was enticing to me.

I honestly don't think Pam ever really cared about material wealth. But as our experiences carried us deeper into this world where people had more money than they could ever use in a lifetime, we could see that none of them were as happy as we were, and we were quite poor by their standards.

It just seemed that they were always seeking an advantage over others, and no matter how much wealth they had, it was never enough. It appeared to us that life for them was a competition. Whoever has the most was the winner. I heard many times, "Whoever dies with the most toys wins."

Pam and I talked about this a lot, even when we were living in the hearse, and we came to the conclusion that having a lot of money made you an asshole. So many of the happiest people we encountered were poor in material wealth.

Early on, we came up with the idea that if we could meet one, just one wealthy person who was as happy as we were, that we would change our belief around money. The world appeared so messed up that we truly believed that we would die young.

I made it through Vietnam, and Pam survived New York, but Civil Rights, Women's Rights, our gay and lesbian friends suffering, the suffering of the poor, continuing war, and the general condition of society just made us feel that life like this was unsustainable, and that we would never reach 30 years old. So, we decided to "retire" early.

We just quit, dropped out, disappeared from "normal" life. This lifestyle continued until we had 4 children, became "home owners," quit drugs, and at 40 we looked at each other and said, "Uh oh, we didn't die, what do we do now?" We finally got a bank account...at 40. And that's when I created the job of IT consultant, and began to work for myself, and Pam's beading business was going well. We still believed that money was bad, but we had to have some to survive. Just enough to get by.

We had a friend who had gone from no money to making millions of dollars, and was doing wonderful things. They were incredibly successful in business and gave away a lot of their money for causes that they believed in, not just for tax write offs. So, we decided to have a talk with them about money. They had material wealth and were also happy. We asked about how this worked.

The essence of the conversation went like this. "Money is neither good nor bad. It is just energy, green energy. And like all energy, it is available to use. The important thing is not to try to dam up the flow. Allow yourself to become a channel for money and let it flow through you, without holding on, or trying to hold it. Open yourself to the flow and don't try to hoard it.

First, it is important to "prime the pump," by giving away that which you think you don't have enough of and allow it to be replaced. In other words, share unconditionally what you have. So, we started practicing that idea. Pam never went by a homeless person or someone needing money without giving some.

We started to work together to sneak money into people's pockets or purses so that they would discover it, and not know where it came from. That was important. To give without seeking acknowledgement, and without expecting any kind of result or judgement about how they would use the money.

It became a game for us, and money did begin to flow. At least it felt better. This was also the time when Pam was introduced to Transformational Breathwork. She was working part time at a metaphysical bookstore and there was a group of women participating in breathwork sessions and told Pam that she should come to the group and try it out.

She didn't feel comfortable in a group setting, and she didn't have the money to spend on the session. She asked the facilitator if she would be willing to trade for some of her beaded earrings. The facilitator told her that she would trade for two sessions, and after that Pam would have enough money to pay in cash. Pam did this first session with the intent of increasing our financial flow. Now I didn't participate, but after that first session, our income doubled.

After the second session, it doubled again, and Pam was now paying in cash for the sessions. After some time, she came to me and said she wanted to become a breathwork facilitator, that this is the work she was supposed to do. I agreed to pretty much anything she wanted to do, so I was all in.

The training was expensive and took a year. We didn't have the money, but Pam kept calling them and asking for a scholarship. They finally relented and gave her a partial scholarship, and she began her training. They would meet for three days for intensive training, and then would have "homework" for several months, and then meet again. It was certainly life changing. I'm realizing this is getting long, and there's much more to tell about this, so I'm going to stop for now and continue tomorrow.

May 14, 2022

When Pam began breathwork in earnest, everything in our lives changed. She knew that this was the missing piece in her work as a healer, therapist, comforter, and path walker. She felt she had found her life's purpose. To help others any way she could, and breathwork was the quickest, most direct way to shift people's emotions and energy. She called it the "Hotline to God."

When she finally got her partial scholarship to the teaching program, she was ecstatic. I mentioned before, the teaching consisted of four 3-day weekend intensive meetings, and months of homework in between. A year in total. The lessons consisted of a considerable amount of information about anatomy and mechanics of breathing, and also a LOT of breathwork sessions. They would do one session after the other for the three days. When she would return from her weekends, she would be as light filled and high frequency as any time we ever did acid.

While doing these sessions, the students were processing their own internal fears, phobias, issues from childhood, held thoughtforms, and anything else that would prevent them from becoming the best person that they could be. For anyone who has not experienced breathwork, it is intense. It is an hour of continuous, deep circular breathing and hyper oxygenation of the body. She never liked it when I compared it to tripping, but there are a lot of similarities.

Her last weekend's training came around, and she was sick. She was vomiting, and feeling light, so she called the facilitator and told her that she could not come, that she was ill. The facilitator told her that this was just her resistance to completing the training, and the class would wait until she got there. Pam told them she didn't think she could do it, and they told her to get in the car and drive over there, that this was purely her resistance and fear of moving forward, and that the entire class would wait for her to arrive.

She got up, and drove the hour to the training site, stopping several times to throw up. When she arrived, they immediately began the breathing sessions. When she felt nauseous, the assistants would roll her over, let her throw up, and then continue breathing.

After the first day, she was no longer sick, and had made whatever breakthrough that was necessary for her to continue. This whole process was miraculous and gave her great personal confidence and increased her desire to carry this wonderful tool to as many people as she could.

After her certification, she began running breathwork workshops. I was her assistant. We had a circuit of a number of towns where she developed groups that wanted to breathe once a month, so we traveled to each of these towns on a regular basis running the workshops. It never failed to amaze me to watch the transformation of these people in each session.

As her confidence in herself, and the process increased she became bolder in where she would run the workshops. We were also still working with music in prisons, so she decided to do some breathwork with the inmates. In this one maximum security facility, the warden was so impressed by our music, and the effect it had on the inmates who attended our prison concerts and teaching, that he said we could do pretty much anything we wanted, so breathwork was approved.

She promoted it in the prison as a way to "get high" without drugs, and it was free. They liked that idea, and when the time came to do the presentation, there was a full house for the session. Quite a number of the attendees were young, cocky gang members, and I was a bit nervous. Actually, quite a bit nervous. I mean this was my wife in a room full of 30 or so inmates, and she was going to carry them into a breath session. She was fearless.

Part of the instruction for the breath is to get the breath into the belly, or belly breath, using the diaphragm, and then move the breath into the mid, or heart region, and then further up into the upper lungs. She watched them breathe and kept telling them they weren't getting the full belly breath. So, she walked up to one of the main young black men, pulled open his overcoat, and reached in and put her hand on his stomach with the instruction to "Breathe into my hand!"

There was a lot of gasping in the room, and his eyes became as large as saucers. A small hesitation, and then he began to start breathing into his belly. It was a major breakthrough, and there was applause from a lot of the inmates, and also some nervous laughter, but when they saw this guy doing it, they all began to try.

Breathwork is an amazing thing. It often brings about tears with emotional release, but it can also create laughter in abundance as the frequency of the oxygenation takes place. There in the prison, behind those bars and walls, in that room, both were occurring.

There were tears, there was laughter, and just for a while love overcame fear. They really liked it. The giddy feeling of hyperoxygenation made them feel lighter, and sort of like taking drugs. Pam always emphasized that if you would just take 100 circular breaths each day, that it would change your life. We returned to the prison to do the breath workshops with them quite a few times, and always with great success.

We also offered a meditation class to teach them how to move into a no-mind state of rest and rejuvenation. When we arrived to teach the first class, there were 13 guys in the room from all kinds of "groups." There were Christian, Muslim, Jewish, Pagan men, Wiccan men and pretty much any other group you can imagine.

We began to talk and describe the process, and they basically told us they already knew how to meditate, so we suggested that we just meditate together for the class. They liked that idea, so we settled in to meditate together.

In a flash, all of these guys were gone. They immediately went into deep meditation and were gone. Meanwhile both Pam and I were having great difficulty achieving the meditative state, and we thought we were seasoned meditators. But the noise and distractions!!! There were loud clanging doors, loud announcements on the PA system, loud conversations, and some arguments among other inmates who were nearby, but not part of the class. In a word, there was not one second of silence. It was so, so hard, but we finally managed to get into deep meditation.

The most difficult thing was to get them to come back. After we finished meditating, we said to them, "Holy crap guys. We thought we were teaching the class, but you have schooled us! What is up with this?" They said it was the only way they could get out of the prison and the noise, that the lack of silence in the facility was one of the most difficult issues with their incarceration. They said that there was not a time, 24/7, when there was not noise like that.

That became a major teaching point in all of our classes from that point on. When people would complain that they couldn't meditate, or focus on breathing because the refrigerator made noise, or there was someone mowing the lawn, or there was a truck or plane passing by, we would tell them the story of these dedicated inmates. Then we would instruct them to hone their focus. It didn't always work with "free" people. They have so many distractions. Yeah, right.

May 15, 2022

In 1987 when we had the Harmonic Convergence gathering at our place, one of the events that took place was the sweat lodge. That first sweat lodge had power, but honestly it was somewhat pathetic also. We were white people trying to create a sacred Native American ceremony. We had been given permission by the Chief to do it, with basic instruction, but we were infants in the world of genuine Spiritual Ceremony.

The lodge itself was okay and I built the fire up to heat the rocks, but we never really achieved the heat and intensity of what we later learned was a real Sweat Lodge Ceremony. Nor did we know there were more types of Lodges with greater purposes than just getting inside a dark enclosure and sweating.

No, a genuine Sweat Lodge is not a sauna, it is a sacred, transformational experience. But we sincerely tried. We didn't know all the rules, but we were given strict instructions that women who were menstruating were not allowed in, or near, the Lodge. Actually, in some traditions, men and women are not allowed to participate at the same time. Women have power. Women who are menstruating have great power. The power of the blood, and of the mystery of the creative womb. The sacred place of creation.

There were several women present who wanted to participate in the Lodge, but were in their monthly time, and were excluded. They asked Pam if it was possible to have a Moon Lodge, which is a Sweat Lodge that is only for women in their time. At a Moon Lodge, no men are present, and only women run the Ceremony. We had not heard of such a thing, but Pam was very open to the idea, and agreed.

Again, I don't know how that first Moon Lodge went, but after that Pam said that it was extremely powerful, and she thought that she should begin to have women's empowerment weekends at our place. That seed created a 13-year period of her Women's Gatherings.

She gathered together a circle of 7 women facilitators from various spiritual traditions and different skills to coordinate these gatherings. It was to be a primitive experience, deep in the forest, where they would camp from Friday afternoon until Sunday afternoon.

There were some rules. There would be no coming and going, once the circle was gathered, no one could leave, or if for some reason they did leave, they could not return for that ceremony. There would be absolutely no drugs or alcohol permitted of any kind, and no pets. For many of the gatherings, no talk was allowed, except at meals, no chatting, which squanders the gathering of Spiritual Energy. A silent retreat.

This would be a deeply personal and spiritual gathering with much emotional and deep personal growth. Private. No males of any kind would be allowed, which meant that after preparing the grounds, I would take my 4 male sons, and leave for the weekend. I knew that many of these women had never camped before, much less peed in the forest, so there was a great deal of fear and hesitation in many of the participants. I tried to make the latrines as comfortable as possible, but they were still latrines.

I can't relate what went on during those weekends, I can just say that when I returned, I could feel the power and change that had occurred. I know they always ended with a Women's Lodge on Saturday night, and these Lodges were deep, real, and Sacred. By this time, Pam and I had participated in several authentic Native Sweat Lodges, some so hot that we had to stick our faces in the dirt of the Earth to get breath, and we learned that if done properly, you didn't just sweat and cleanse, you had visions and spiritual insights. True Sweat Lodges are as powerful as any LSD experience I ever had.

These weekend events continued frequently for 13 years. After 10 years, the facilitators decided it was time for the weekends to include men, and the first gatherings were held that would include both men and women. Pam was concerned that the men who attended would be disruptive, and not as Spiritually focused as the women. She was surprised that the men who came were sincere, gentle and fully present for the experience. There was much healing of the rift between male and female energy.

These 7 women facilitators were so powerful as a group. Their focus and clarity of intent, and hard work was inspirational to me, even just watching from my vantage point outside the circle. They were always so thankful to me for my work in the preparation of the grounds, and physical labor involved in getting it ready for the women. It was such an honor to be involved in this way.

Slowly, over the years, the 7 facilitators began to die, or drift away to other duties, and in the end, there were 4, and finally, the work was done, the changes had been initiated, and the next phase beginning. There would still be gatherings and workshops, but the time of the Women's Empowerment Weekends was finished.

There was a level of sadness at the end, but also a great amount of pride in what had been accomplished. I believe that many, many women's lives were enriched by those experiences, and Pam certainly grew enormously, both Spiritually, and physically, from the primitive nature of the events. The return of the balance of feminine and masculine is absolutely essential if we are to survive as a species.

I'm so proud of the progress of women since the 60's, which is when I became aware of the struggle for balance. I'm also proud of the progress of a lot of men as well, but there is a quite a way to go yet. Pam's physical time for creating change and encouraging women to push for equality and balance is over now, but I hope that those she taught and the work she did will help in continuing the birth into a new era of balance and harmony between men and women and all races.

She often said that there is only one issue in the world, and it's a spiritual one. Our separation from God. The feeling that we are separate. And that issue must be remedied before any political or personal solution can be achieved. We are in fact One. Any small act of kindness for one is an act of kindness for all. Any growth for one is growth for all. Any harm to one is harm to all.

One thing we learned from the Women's Weekends is that when we choose to heal our own lives from past trauma, or familial trauma is that we heal those things for our entire lineage. For our mothers, grandmothers, fathers, grandfathers, all the way back to our distant past, as well as for our children and their children on into the unforeseen future. Practice kindness and unconditional Love, it's really what we are here to do.

Donald T. McMahon

May 17, 2022

It's very early morning. I didn't sleep much last night. The time for Pam's Celebration Of Life is approaching, and the significance and gravity of that milestone is weighing on me. Not in a bad way, but like gravity, relentless and inevitable. I'm zeroing in on a date, which will be soon, but I don't know the place yet. I believe that it's too large for Heartspace. When I am confident, I will announce it, and try to let everyone who is interested in attending know the details.

Relationship. I began this Facebook wandering with Pam's passing. After my announcement on Facebook that, in fact, the rumors of her death were true, I received such a tidal wave of messages, phone calls, and responses, that I was overwhelmed. I had no idea of the size and impact of her life on so many people.

In all those communications, two things kept popping up. One, people were asking me to write something about our life, and two, explain how it was possible to maintain a loving relationship and marriage for over 50 years. That's how this series of posts started. Then it developed a life of its own, and now I am along for the ride for as long as words keep falling onto the page.

When a couple is married for 20 years with 4 children, their relationship takes a back seat for quite a while. The children's needs and daily chores are all consuming, and there are lots of held resentments and unfulfilled expectations in the marriage.

We were preparing for our 20th anniversary when the cracks in our relationship started to appear. We thought we were going to renew our vows and have this big gathering to witness the event. We had invited people from all over. Many musicians that we had shared music experiences with as well as friends and neighbors.

Then, about three or four weeks before the event, we began to argue. "Remember when you said you were going to do this, and you never did?" "Remember when you said you would never do this, and you did?" "Why are you doing that?" "This doesn't make me happy!" "Why are we doing this?"

It kept building. Soon we were asking each other if, in fact, instead of renewing our vows, maybe we actually needed to get a divorce. It had reached a critical phase when we decided we had to do something or separate.

We locked ourselves in a small room in the house with the intention that by the time we left this room, either we were going to have resolved ALL the issues, or we were going to split up, whatever that meant.

There was a lot of crying, screaming at each other and a lot of thoughtless words were said. Finally, she asked me, "Do you even still Love me?" I replied that I did Love her but did not like the way we were relating to each other. She said, "Well I still Love you too, and if our marriage is going to survive, we have to work this out." For three days, we stayed in that room. The children were so concerned that they brought food to us while we were in there. We barely slept. This was all consuming.

Somewhere in the process we realized that we needed to communicate more effectively, because we were saying things we didn't mean, and we were always on defense, and attacking each other. So, we started working on conscious languaging.

I would say something, and she would listen, not interrupting. Then she would repeat back to me what she heard. And I would say something like, "That's not what I said," and she would say, "That's what I heard." Then I would try to convey my thoughts using different words, and the process would repeat. Often it took quite a few tries before what she heard was actually what I was trying to say.

It worked the same way with her speaking and me replying with what I heard. Eventually we reached a point where we achieved actual communication. For example, I grew up in a household where men did not go in the kitchen. That was women's work. And at one point Pam asked me, "Why don't you ever do the dishes?" This is embarrassing for me to say now, but I replied in full innocence and honesty, "What dishes?"

There was an explosion from her with so many expletives that I can't put them in this post. "WHAT DO YOU MEAN WHAT DISHES? THE DISHES THAT ARE HERE AFTER EVERY MEAL. *****##### ARE YOU ###*** BLIND?" and so on for a while. I was shocked that I could be that ignorant and insensitive.

I told her that I Loved her more than life, and I would do ANYTHING she asked me to do, but I was not good at intuiting what she wanted or expected. There was some, "If you really Love me, then you would see these things."

We arrived at the conclusion that women were very intuitive, and men were not. I don't know how this works with other couples, but this was where we arrived. So, we began with each of us clearly laying out simple things that we wanted the other to do, and that helped tremendously.

We also began to realize that we were trapped in the Archetype of Marriage. We had gotten married in a church by a minister, so our paperwork would be complete so we could get additional benefits on the GI Bill for school. We didn't really believe that the words we spoke in that ceremony carried much actual weight. They do.

When we got married, we became part of a "club" of everyone who has ever spoken vows and become "married." The Archetype of Marriage. It's big, it's old, and it's real. We realized that we had outgrown the traditional concept of marriage. Even with all its aspects, it was too small for us.

We decided to end that marriage and start a new one. One that would fit our growing understanding of marriage. We released each other from all vows and prior commitments, and the marriage that had existed before was dissolved. We created a ceremony to finalize it. Our new marriage was based on two simple things. One, that we would always tell each other the truth as best we could see it, because after all, truth is a moving target.

And two, that we would trust each other, so that if one said to the other that their actions or speech were outside of that truth, that we would accept that what they were seeing was their truth, and they were not trying to gain some kind of advantage.

This usually meant that one of us was slipping into some loss of honesty or integrity, and we needed to examine our behavior. Fortunately, it was a rare event that both of us had lost our bearings, but we were still able to work it out because we were focused on the truth at all times.

There were no secrets in our marriage. This was not about sex. Neither of us ever had any kind of affair in our entire marriage. We were free to Love everyone, but sex with anyone else was a line that we would not cross. Monogamy worked for us.

After that day, we began to celebrate unnaversaries instead of anniversaries. Our relationship and marriage grew beyond all of the boundaries of traditional marriage into a brand new form of commitment. It just got better and better, all the way to the "Death do us part" thing.

May 18, 2022

I think the early morning is my favorite time of day. It's quiet and most of the chores and intrusions of the day are far away yet. My mind wanders around a lot in the promise and newness of this time.

I'm still here. I'm thankful that I'm still here, and still wondering why. The great majority of my life was centered around Pam. For more than 50 years we were one being, PamAndDon. With her physical presence gone I'm having difficulty finding myself.

I know we are Spiritually connected, but I continue to be in a state of shock, and the greater part of the day, I'm just lost, unable to find focus. When I do my computer work, it is a familiar state of knowing what to do. When I play music for an audience, I'm able to momentarily move into a sweet familiar realm where for a moment I'm carried into the realm where music sooths me, and in my head and heart I can hear her harmonies quite clearly and feel her close. Music has always been a very intimate experience with us, and somehow it still is.

The rest of the days and nights are filled with confusion and just a general feeling of not knowing what to do next. I have decided that the Celebration of Her Life will be on June 22, 2022. That's all I know. I don't know where it's going to take place yet. I know that she did not want a traditional memorial service. She just wanted a gathering of joy where there was music, and everyone just loved and comforted one another. I don't know how to do that yet, but I trust that Spirit will guide me as always if I can just shut up and listen. When I know more, I will let you know.

Yesterday I wrote about Relationship, and mentioned some of the things that I did that created some of the tensions in our marriage, but I failed to talk about any of the things that she did. It is important to tell this part because it's never one person's fault that a relationship falters.

When we were dialoging and processing, she asked me about the dishes among other things. There was a point where I asked her why she talked so mean to me. She said, "What are you talking about, I never talk mean to you." I said, "Would you allow me to lovingly remind you each time you start talking to me that way?" and she said, "Of course." It took less than a few hours before she said, "Holy crap! You can stop reminding me now, I can see it, and I will work on that."

She didn't know why or when she started a habit of talking mean or in a condescending way, but it had crept into our daily lives as an ugly irritation. I think exhaustion, and the 24/7 responsibility of parenting just took its toll on the manner of conversation. Oddly, I see a lot of parallels in society right now because of the isolation and pressures and strains of the pandemic and world events.

We also realized that we had to take time to nurture and rekindle our relationship that had been put on hold while we were parenting. We started to take one day a week that was "date day." Pretty much whatever else was happening, we began to take a day off for ourselves. Mostly it was just taking time out to share a meal together and practice communicating in a loving way.

Relationships require constant care, just like a garden. It's not possible to expect it to produce a fruitful harvest if you just plant the seeds excitedly in the beginning and then let weeds and lack of water reduce it to a brush pile that needs to be scraped down and burned. It takes work...lots of work....constant effort and work.

The fact that both of us were willing to look at and be reminded of our "bad" behaviors toward each other allowed us to work through them and replace them with loving behavior. If each of us had not been able to stop and look at and accept our part in the difficulties we were having, then the relationship would have ended and we would have missed out on the very best parts, the parts where everyone looked at us and said, "Your relationship is so wonderful. That's what we want."

One time we were in a restaurant having lunch, and there was a table next to us with three women who were laughing and talking and obviously having some kind of friends reunion. At some point, they called over to us and told us how beautiful we looked, and so happy. They began a conversation with us that progressed to us telling the story of the dissolving of our marriage and the creation of the new one. At the end, one of the women was responding to the part of the story where I said, "What dishes?" and she had tears in her eyes and she said, "Yes, I wish someone had told me this story earlier. I threw away a 30-year marriage because he didn't put his dirty socks in the hamper. Maybe if I had just told him, we could have saved our relationship."

Please, please, please, let's all find a way to listen and talk to each other in a kind and loving way. I know that ultimately, we all want the same things in our lives. It's not easy, but if you are really in Love, all of the work, pain and suffering is worth it. At least that's the way I see it.

The First 60 Days

May 19, 2022

There was a young woman who managed to find her way to us. She was a runaway and had managed to live on her own since she was 16, I think, maybe younger.

After escaping from her very fundamentalist Christian family, she hoboed for several years, meaning she just hopped freight trains and rode. She traveled all over the United States, and up into Canada. I can't remember how old she was when she appeared at our home, but she was still under 18. She was of Nordic genetics, tall and blonde/brunette, and very muscular from living on the road. Lots of tattoos and piercings adorned her body and face, and her tattoos were not the butterflies, rainbows, and unicorn kind, but skulls, skeletons, barbed wire and frightening images. Some of the tattoos were more like prison, self-made tattoos, and the piercings ranged from small to large D rings with big nails hanging from her ears.

There was a lot of pain exhibited in this child. Often when we saw her, she was wearing combat boots, old army fatigues, often with black lace on her arms and legs. She was slender, but tall, and appeared like someone you really didn't want to have as your enemy. She drank a lot. Mostly vodka and hard whiskey. There was something about her that was so incredibly beautiful, and sad.

She and Pam talked a lot, and with me as well, but not like they did. Pam had this way with people. She was a Universal Mother and all people felt safe and comforted by her. They tended to open up their darkest secrets and greatest pain, and she had the perfect words to soothe them and get them to remove their masks and armor and show her their truth.

This child had endured more pain and hardship than any child should have to experience. Like so many, she sort of became an adopted daughter who passed in and out of our lives at her choosing. After some time, Pam was curious about how a young woman could travel the way she did, and in the company that she kept, and not be physically harmed. Her answer was one of the most perfect pieces of wisdom to come our way. She said, "It's easy. You just never talk about the unholy trinity. Sex, politics, or religion. If you never talk about these things, you never have trouble."

This piece of information hit us broadside and was such a revelation. Without those three topics, there is so much that we can agree on. In my rambling posts, I will probably venture into all three. She told us lots of stories of her life on the road, and eventually her early life and the reasons for running away.

One day she called us from somewhere out in the world, and asked if she could come to have her 18th birthday at our house. She said it was an important milestone and she didn't have any other place that she would rather be for it, than with us. It turned out to be a wild and crazy time with lots of street kids and vagabonds of all kinds, but overall, it was good, and we survived.

Later, she asked Pam if she would officiate her marriage. Pam agreed, and she had her wedding at our home, in the woods. Again, her wedding party was a group of homeless, street people, and friends. I gathered those in attendance together at the fire circle and since they were already drinking, I gave a little speech about the woods being our church, and the ceremony of marriage was sacred and respect for both the church and the ceremony were expected. They were not to drink while we went further into the woods to the spot where the marriage would happen, and there would be silence while we walked the several hundred yards from the fire circle to the wedding place. It took some tough talk on my part, but it worked. They all left their various drinks at the fire circle, became quiet, and walked reverently to the "altar."

After we were assembled and waiting, Pam came through the woods, and winding down the hill, escorting the bride dressed in homemade white lace and satin from the thrift store, and she was still wearing combat boots. She was beautiful, and all the people assembled were quiet and deeply affected by the loveliness of the moment. There were birds singing, and turtles had shown themselves as witnesses.

I am certain there has never been a more meaningful and blessed wedding. When the marriage ceremony was complete, there was much cheering and celebration as we all proceeded back to the fire circle, with a bonfire, hot dogs, marshmallows, and beer and vodka. What a wedding feast. We talked and talked with them all about their lives, and their dreams. Even the homeless and gypsies have dreams.

Eventually it wound down and they all slowly disappeared into the forest, and further into the world. Other than the bride, we never saw any of them again, but they definitely left an impression. She and her husband were living in a school bus in Oregon, when she called and told us she was pregnant with her second child, and would it be possible to come to our place to give birth. There were issues with their current living situation, and she said that we were the only place where she felt safe enough to birth this next child.

Of course, Pam agreed, and she arrived, very pregnant, and with a two-year-old son. The father had stayed behind to bring the bus later. Births are always amazing events. We had an old step van in the woods behind our house. After it was no longer functional as a vehicle, I parked it up on blocks, and in the beginning, I turned it into a makeshift recording studio, and later modifications turned it into the Love Shack, where Pam and I could escape from the multitudes of kids and have romantic rendezvous. It was here that her child was born.

She was amazing in the birth process. She had a midwife, and Pam and I were in attendance. It turned out to be one of the hottest days we had experienced in a long time. It was over 100 degrees, and very humid.

There was no air conditioning in the Love Shack. Sweat was the word of the day. Even without the birthing work, everyone was just sweating so heavily that it was like being in a shower. So, she was REALLY sweating with the hard work of labor.

Why is it that no matter how many times you see it, the miracle of birth ALWAYS brings tears. A new life, a new beautiful girl child, and a beaming, tired, exhausted mother in a step van in the woods. Life really is a wonderous thing. She went on to have two more children.

Sadly, the marriage failed, and ended not in a pretty way. Pam counselled them for nearly a year before they finally gave up. After the separation, we lost touch for a couple of years. She just disappeared. We tried many times to find her, with no success.

A couple of days after Pam's passing, she showed up at the door with a couple of dozen eggs as a gift. We hugged and cried a lot, and she apologized for not being in touch, it was just too painful. But she is a survivor and continues to work for the success of her children.

After a great deal of talk with Pam, she had managed to reconcile with her birth mother and family before her own divorce. There is nothing that Love cannot overcome. Sometimes a marriage is just not supposed to work. But the children are all amazing, and I feel like they, along with all the other new beings coming in, will make this place better somehow. At least that's my daily prayer.

May 20, 2022

Last night was the first of the hot, humid, still, southern nights for this year. It was 82 degrees at midnight, and absolutely still with not a breath of moving air. We always tried to avoid air conditioning whenever we could. We leave the windows open, and sometimes even the doors open to receive the cool night air, and the sounds of the creatures of the darkness.

There were times when we were living in the bus that we would get up in the middle of the night and take a cold shower to make it comfortable enough to go to bed. We grew up in Columbia, SC without air conditioning. In the 1940's and 1950's there really wasn't any widespread use of anything other than window fans, or these big ceiling exhaust fans that would draw cool air in at night.

I can remember nights when I was a child where I would stick my face up against the window to receive the breeze created by the exhaust fan. Or sometimes, and Pam remembered this as well, we would get out of bed and lay on the floor, because the floor felt cooler.

A couple of years ago, I ran into a couple at the local peach stand while I was buying the caviar that is South Carolina peaches. It was a sweltering day, nearing 100, and so humid that standing still created streams of sweat down my face. In a brief chat, they asked where I was from, and I told them that I was born and raised in Columbia. They guy said, "Oh yes, Columbia. Do you know what the difference is between Columbia and Hell?" and I said I did not. He said, "A screen door."

Growing up there prepared me for military training at Fort Polk, Louisiana, and subsequent deployment to Vietnam. Learning to go to sleep wet, and wake up wetter, and how to breathe air so full of humidity that it felt similar to drowning. You get used to it so much that our travels in the desert would make our skin crack, and when we would get off the plane on our return, when we stepped outside I think you could hear the sucking sound of our skin re-moisturizing, and it felt good to breathe water again.

It gets hot and humid here in Green Creek as well, but nothing like Columbia. In the first few years that we lived here, the windows had no screens, but that was alright because we also had no mosquitos. The mosquitos came later and arrived on the rains of a tropical storm. They have since taken up residence and multiplied, so that screens are essential. I put in ceiling fans early on to create some air movement both in the summer, and to move the heat from the woodstove throughout the house.

There were nights before we had screens, when a bat or two would find their way into our bedroom and be unable to find their way out. Pam would wake me up telling me in a hushed but intense voice, "DONALD T....THERE'S A BAT IN THE HOUSE!!!!!" Sometimes they would collide with the ceiling fan, and knock them across the room, but usually I was able to get up and escort them to the open windows.

You can do this by holding up a sheet or cloth, and pretend to be a wall. Their sonar perceives the sheet as solid and they avoid it, allowing you to guide them. We like bats. They eat mosquitos.

Pam was so sensitive to all creatures. We almost never dispatched any living being. We relocated bees, spiders, birds, bats, snakes, frogs, or any other creature to the outside without harm. There was this one night, the night of the rat. There are rats here. Not the city rats, but field rats that have been living here long before us. Sometimes they would find their way in.

Especially in the beginning, before I was able to completely rodent proof the house. If they were especially persistent in coming in at night, I felt I had to trap them. So, I got the big rat trap and set it before we went to bed.

Shortly after the lights went out, I heard it snap loudly, and knew it had done its job. Then I heard the noise of the trap flapping about. It had caught the rat, but not killed it. This went on for a few minutes, and then it got quiet, so we went to sleep thinking that I would take it out in the morning.

Pam woke me from a deep, dead sleep, again in a hushed, but intense voice, "DONALD T...THERE'S A RAT ON MY BACK!!" I immediately went from sound asleep to very wide awake. She was sitting up in the bed and I could see her silhouetted against the window, and there was a large rat hanging on her back. Its head was just behind her neck, and the body was long enough with the tail to reach her butt.

The vision of this sent me into full blown PTSD, and I instinctually struck out with my fist, and hit the rat, knocking it off of Pam and into the wall and then the floor. It scurried into the closet, and I quickly shut the closet door, confining the rat to the closet.

But by now, I was no longer in Green Creek, I was fully transported back to Vietnam and had completely lost myself. I could hear the sounds, feel the heat, and the smells. The smells are the most intense. Somewhere, way off in the distance I could hear Pam's voice, "Donald T., it's alright. Feel my hands. Look at your feet. You're not there, you're here and right now, right here everything is okay." It took a while, but slowly I was able to focus on our bedroom, and Pam's loving embrace, holding me close.

I don't know how other veterans, who don't have a Pam, are able to cope when this happens. And I know it does. I was shaking so much that I could not stand up. Then there was the rat in the closet. Pam said it was locked in the closet, and couldn't get out, so we could deal with it in the morning. There was very little sleep that night, waiting for the morning with dread.

As soon as it was light, I got a large trash can and put it by the closet door, and very cautiously opened it. There was the rat. Not some horrible gutter rat, but a beautiful field rat, cowering in the corner. I coaxed her into the can, to remove her from the house. She had a bloody nose but seemed otherwise unharmed.

Then I began to examine the bedroom scene. I found the trap in the other room, and there was a slight trail of blood from there to our bedroom, up the bedspread, across my body, and ending at Pam. Then I got it.

The rat was coming to Pam for healing and comfort in the same way that I was. It was somehow attracted to her healing presence. And I had reacted with violence. It was a big lesson. I realized that I was the rat, injured and cornered in the closet of my mind, and there was Pam. Always a healing presence. Always able to calm and soothe. She was selfless and gave to anyone and everyone that crossed her path. And somehow, she chose me as her partner. I released the rat outside, with blessings. I have recalled that lesson many, many times since then, and am so very thankful.

May 21, 2022

Things are different now. I'm sleeping in our bed again. There is no longer the nightly waking at 2 or 3 to wait for 3:35, the moment of her last breath. Most nights not waking until 5 or 6. Even Kiki has stopped coming in to lick my face and wake me up early. I think maybe there is less salt in my tears for her to get from my cheeks. The ophthalmologist has me putting these "fake tear drops" in my eyes because they are dry. I told her I'm just dehydrated from continuous crying.

I have only had two dreams since she transitioned. They were both very intense and realistic. I could feel and touch her in my dreams. The first one was maybe six weeks ago. It wasn't pleasant. We were having a disagreement in that dream. I was upset because I felt she was abandoning me again. I kept telling her that she had left me to marry her first husband, and she had deserted me when I was in Vietnam, and now she had abandoned me again. I was angry.

She kept telling me that she had not left me, that she was as close to me now as she had ever been. She said there were things she had to do that required her to leave her physical body, but that she was still with me. I was still angry. When I woke up, I was sobbing. I knew it was right, but I didn't like it, and all I could do was cry, sometimes shouting to Spirit, or Pam, or whoever was listening, asking what I was supposed to do now.

But, you know, daylight comes, and non-dream life comes back in with the sunrise. Just make breakfast, make the bed, wash my face, get dressed, and take a breath and the first step of the day. Then one task after another begins to appear, just like always.

In the second dream, which was only a few weeks ago, it was even more realistic, but I was no longer angry, I was just sad and depressed. Pam came in so clearly and held me. In that way she had of always telling me that "right now, right here, everything is alright," she calmed me and told me, "It was okay to be sad for a while, but don't dwell there. Don't make sadness my new home. Just remember that in Truth, I am as close to you now as I have ever been. Love doesn't die with the body, it's eternal."

I have to keep reminding myself of this message, over and over and over again. I'll have to say that it has helped me get through most days. There are still those triggers that cause me to fall into a dark hole for hours, and maybe a day at a time, but they are less frequent. Sometimes a simple word, phrase, image, or sound will kick off a flood of tears, and I never know when it will be. I believe this is normal with Transition and Great Love.

I know that I am blessed enough to be part of a Great Love, and a witness to the Great Awakening of Love in this world. I'm also aware that it is difficult to see at this moment, but it IS here. We are ALL witnesses. It's all of our work to bear witness to this blossoming of Love. Love your neighbor. Love your enemy. Do good to those who spitefully use you. Visit the sick. Visit those in prison. Welcome the stranger. Give comfort to those in need. These are not just empty words to me, and Pam's life gave new importance and meaning to these concepts for me. I AM SO THANKFULL!!!.

This was not what I intended to write about this morning. In fact, I never know what's going to spill out. My conscious mind tells me one thing, and then something else appears on the page and I just have to roll with it. I don't want to sound like a preacher. This whole exercise is about Pam's life, our story, told through my filter. If God's willing and the creek don't rise, I'll continue with the story soon.

May 22, 2022

Kiki did wake me up this morning, but not at an unreasonable hour, and she didn't lick my face.

Once Pam became a Transformational Breathwork Facilitator, she really kicked things into a high gear. She became an evangelist for breathing, and I became her assistant. When she did private sessions, they were private, I did not assist, but when she did group breathing sessions, she wanted me to help.

Group breath sessions generally took place on a weekend, and we would travel to various cities, and she had a pretty regular clientele for monthly group sessions. Often when doing these group sessions, multiple people would "activate" at the same time, and Pam could not get to everyone in a timely manner. This is where I came in.

Breath sessions could become extremely intense, with lots of crying, laughing, and emotional releasing. Pam always knew exactly how to handle these situations. Over years, she taught me, but I was never as effective as she was, but I got better.

Sometimes she would teach mini-breaths in a conference or retreat. Mostly she would get people to pay attention to their breath, and just for a little while, to try to breathe deeper. What we found was that most people today are hardly breathing at all. There are lots of reasons for this, which she would talk about in her presentations, but mainly we quit fully breathing to "protect" ourselves from trauma.

We come into this world on an in-breath, and we leave this world on an exhale. Believe me, I have witnessed both. We often say something was so bad, or shocking, or even wonderful, that it "took my breath away." By the time most of us are adults, we are just breathing heads.

Pam would gently invite people to be aware of their breath, and gradually expand it to include their belly, mid body, and upper lobes of their lungs. Sometimes it only takes a few breaths for someone to "activate'. In a controlled environment, with a small group of people, this is great. With a large audience....not so much.

The first time "activation" occurs, it can be frightening to some, and it is important to be able to gently assist the person in adjusting to their rediscovered breath. Often this is where I, and "spotters" would jump to service in a large audience. We became quite adept at seeing the first signs of activation and could slow the process down. So, she tailored the large audience presentation so they could experience greater breathing capacity without activating.

She was magnificent to watch as she taught people about breathing. The breathing process that she was taught was a pretty aggressive breathing pattern with the goal of activation and opening the emotional body to healing. Over time, she began to realize that it was not necessary to be so aggressive to achieve the same results.

There was a time when she was invited to participate in a small retreat for women who were in various stages of cancer treatment. Some were still in shock at receiving the initial diagnosis, some were in the painful and difficult period of treatments, and some were on their way to transition when treatment failed. Many of them were frail in both body and mind.

She knew that these women could not do the aggressive breathing pattern, so she instead developed a gentle form of the breathing, with confidence that the breath would do what was necessary for these women. Her experience was that it worked anyway, and so her techniques began to diverge from her formal training. I was in awe of what she was doing. It was so beautiful, and the changes that occurred in people's lives with just a change in breathing was amazing.

Her mother had developed Parkinson's disease. It was a long slow progression over 13 years, the last 3 of which were in a nursing home in Spartanburg, South Carolina. Close enough to us without the paperwork to move her across state lines.

Pam visited her there every day. Sometimes they would just talk, sometimes she would take her to the salon and do her hair, sometimes take her out to "shop," which mostly meant going through the store and feeling the material of every dress.

Pam was looking for some way to ease her mother's suffering, and breathwork was just too much for the nursing home. Plus, her mother was sort of scared of Pam's lifestyle and the rumors of her healing work.

This is when Reiki appeared in our lives. A friend of hers had become a Reiki Master Teacher and was giving her first class and needed some people to attend who would give her honest feedback about her teaching performance, so she asked Pam if she would be one of the students. Pam agreed and it was the first step in a long process of learning Reiki, practicing Reiki, and eventually teaching Reiki.

For those who don't know what Reiki is, Reiki is a process of "laying on of hands," of energy healing. This form came to us through a Japanese teacher and gradually found its way to the West. The term Reiki is composed of two parts, Rei, meaning God or Spirit, and Ki, meaning energy. Ki, or Chi, is just a term for energy, usually associated with personal energy.

In various martial arts forms, students are taught to gather and direct their Ki or Chi in defensive maneuvers. In Reiki, the practitioner opens themselves up as a conduit for Spiritual Energy to flow through. It is quite a powerful and effective process and can be done quietly with nothing more than touching someone or holding hands.

It was a perfect tool for working in the nursing home and with her mother. When I saw the results of what she was doing, I decided to take the training as well. Our teacher at the time operated a Reiki booth at a local festival. It was a big music festival with several stages, food vendors, all sorts of clothing, and festival booths, and there was a section for healing arts. There were massage therapists, yoga teachers, and all sorts of healing booths.

Our teacher had the only Reiki booth, and she asked if we would like to participate. Since the early 70's, we had avoided festivals, and crowds, but we decided to do this one. In the booth, there were 2 massage tables, and we did 20 minute sessions with 2 practitioners at each table. One table was high, and one table was low, so that we could switch off during the day to give our legs a break from standing.

It was truly a transformative experience. For 3 days, we had people lined up at the booth from 9 in the morning until dark. Every 20 minutes, a new person was on the table. Sometimes we would stop for a brief lunch, but mostly we worked straight through.

In the beginning, I was concerned that I wasn't doing the process correctly, because I was so new at this "laying on of hands" thing. It only took about 2 or 3 people before it became automatic, without thought, and like the music we play, if we could just get our personal self out of the way, and let Reiki flow through us, the results were wonderful.

You would think that we would be so tired at the end of these long, busy days, that we would just drop. That was not the case. Usually we were so energized that we would have to go to the main music stage, and dance for an hour just to wind down.

After a couple of years of working with clients with both breathwork and Reiki, Pam decided she wanted to be able to teach Reiki. This started a whole different quest.

May 24, 2022

There are many schools, or lineages of Reiki training, just like there are many schools of breathwork training that have their own particular methods and curricula. After Pam was trained and certified in Level 1 and Level 2 Reiki, she just wanted to use the techniques to help people.

She was focused on private sessions, and began several years as a busy, successful Reiki practitioner, while she continued to study more advanced forms of the process. After a while she began to receive inquiries about teaching. She started looking into becoming certified as a master/teacher.

As always, she researched various schools and training paths to become a teacher. She became trained by a couple of non-affiliated Reiki teachers, but did not feel confident enough in herself to actually start teaching.

One day while she was reading in a magazine about Reiki, she saw a schedule of master/teacher trainings, and saw a picture of this particular woman teacher, Laurelle Shanti Gaia with the International Center For Reiki Training. Pam came to me and said, "I don't know what it is about this person, but I am positive that this is my teacher, and I want to take some training with her." I learned early on to respect Pam's intuition, so I was on board.

The issue was that all of the classes on her schedule were in California, Chicago, Arizona, and we did not have the monetary resources to send Pam to any of those, so she waited. Eventually, there was a class just north of Miami, Florida. We had friends in Miami that we could stay with, and we could drive there, so she signed up for the class.

The class was three days of intensive study, with practice overnight. The traffic in Miami was insane, and she would not drive, so each morning I would drive her the 15 miles up to the class, return to our friend's house, where I spent the days with him, and then I would return in the late afternoon to pick her up. She would eat, and then retire to our bedroom and study. She was so very excited. I could hear in her voice and see in her manner that she was really taken by this teacher.

We didn't have much time together during the training other than the drive up, and the drive back. In the morning of the last day of the class, she asked me to bring my guitar when I came to pick her up, and we would play a couple of songs for them and give them each one of our most recent CD recordings as a gift.

It was a relatively small class and Laurelle was co-teaching the class with her husband, Michael. I didn't know what to expect, so I just did what Pam told me to do, and showed up at the end of the class with my guitar. We started to sing to the class, and Laurelle started to cry. I was afraid I had done something wrong, but we kept playing. We only sang a few songs, because they were on a tight schedule and needed to get to the airport. I was only with them for a very short while, but the meeting was magical, and I felt I had met some old friends.

On the drive back to Green Creek, Pam kept repeating how good the class was, and how thorough and informative it had been. She said that now she felt confident in teaching some classes of her own, and she said she wanted to take some further training with Laurelle. I remember her saying, "This is the way I want to teach."

The First 60 Days

Almost as soon as we had arrived home, Pam's back went out. As a teenager, she had broken her neck while diving from the high diving board and had periodic back problems as a result. This time she was really in a lot of pain.

She kept telling me what the breathwork teachers had told her when she was sick the last day of breathwork training. "This is just resistance to the work. Keep breathing and work through it." A few days into this "back attack," she received a call from Laurelle. Laurelle wondered if we would be interested in coming and singing for the International Reiki Retreat in upstate New York.

Pam was so excited she said we would really like to do that. We didn't know exactly what we were going to do there, but we committed to going and playing music. They called us in March I think, and the retreat was on Labor Day weekend in September, so she had a few months to recover from her back injury, and it took most of it before she was ready to travel.

This was in 2002, the year after the 9/11 attack on New York, and my military awareness was triggered, and I had some concerns about going to New York near the anniversary of that horrible event, but she was determined.

It was a powerful and wonderful event. The moment we started singing, the audience loved us, and we really felt we had found a community of like-minded people and we were comfortable. The workshops were all informative and interesting, and the conversations were uplifting. We made lasting friendships that are still with us today.

Since we were on a tight budget, we had taken a giant cooler of food so we could eat from the car and not have to eat road food. Much of our food was from our garden, lots of homegrown tomatoes. We were sitting in the parking lot, waiting to register, and eating tomato sandwiches when a woman pulled up and came over and told us how beautiful the sandwiches looked. We invited her for lunch and began a conversation.

It turned out that she was the Reiki Coordinator for the hospital in Hartford, Connecticut. This was amazing to us that Reiki was accepted inside the hospital, and she said that any family member, patient, doctor, or staff member could request Reiki, and she would coordinate a practitioner to help them. She said that sometimes surgeons would ask for Reiki to be given to an organ before transplant.

This was all new and exciting to us. We had seen the effects of Reiki on Pam's clients, and our family, but we had no idea of how widespread it had become. When she heard our accent, she told us she was originally from North Carolina. We asked where, and she said, "Oh, it's a little place you have never heard of." She told us the name of the town where she was born, and it was 15 miles from our house.

These types of serendipity were so common, that they ceased to be shocking. At the end of the retreat, Laurelle came to Pam and said, "Will you come and play for every retreat that we have forever?" Pam said, "Sure, but each year you have to call and ask us again." Laurelle asked why, and Pam said, "We don't want you to feel obligated. In the future you might find someone else that you would prefer to play, and that would be alright with us, so we need you to ask us each time."

Every year, we would receive a call from Laurelle, and after her passing, from Michael saying, "This is the call. Would you be willing to play for the retreat this year?" The answer was always yes, and we always laughed and talked for a while.

The upcoming retreat in 2022 would have been our 20th anniversary playing together for the retreat. Michael told me he understood that it might be too emotional and difficult for me to attend this year, but I was welcome to participate in any and all of the events, whether I played or just attended....or not.

I have agreed to go and play and give her presentation on Breathwork and Reiki. I'm not sure how this will work out, but I have total confidence that Pam and Spirit will guide me and give me the words and music to continue and honor her work. It's all an adventure, and we have never been shy about jumping off the ledge.

May 25, 2022

Well, a decision has been made. Pam's Celebration of Life will be from 2 to 4 pm on June 22 at Song Hill Reserve, which is located between Landrum and Gowensville, South Carolina. It's a beautiful place, and they have a great web page if any of you want to see it. There is a short walk from the parking area to the pavilion, but there is a turn around right at the facility where elderly or disabled people can have easy access.

Given that that day is a Wednesday, and we live in a reasonably remote area, and the Pandemic is still lurking around, I have absolutely no idea how many people will choose to attend, so I am making my best guess for the venue. If you do choose to come, please do not wear basic black, wear something colorful and joyful.

Pam's birthday parties began with her 40th in 1985. She always liked seeing old friends and singing and participating in music of all kinds. In the beginning there would be some people who came from far away who would camp overnight, and we would play and drum and chant around the bonfire and generally have a hippie good time. Each year, there would be a few more people, and it would be so much fun.

By the time of her 50th, there were starting to be a couple of hundred attendees, with quite a few camping, and it had grown to Friday through Sunday, with lots of potluck type meals, and community activities.

Her 50th was a "croning ceremony," and there were women from many groups who came to be represented and honor her for becoming a Crone, or Wisdom Woman. She had lived to 50 and through lots of trials and work, had shown herself to be a true Woman of Power.

We did a ceremony where I led all the attendees down through the woods, drumming and chanting to a spot on the creek where there was a small waterfall and a small pool with a large rock in the middle. We called it the "Christening Hole," because quite a few blessings, christenings, and baptisms had occurred there.

After the group had assembled at the creek, Pam came walking barefoot in the creek from further up in the woods, dressed in her most beautiful clothes. She was accompanied by a wonderful woman dressed in green and brown camouflage tights looking like some kind of wood sprite. It was awesome.

Some of the women attendants led me to the rock in the pool to join Pam on the rock. We looked at each other, and spontaneously spoke private words of love and commitment to each other, and just stood for a moment, or a lifetime, lost in Love.

There were some words spoken by the women congratulating and honoring Pam for achieving crone status, and then the group of attendees made a tunnel with their bodies and outstretched hands through which Pam and I walked, receiving blessings from everyone there, and then we proceeded back to the bonfire, and the party continued.

Ceremony has always been an important part of our lives. There should be ceremonies marking different parts of life. When girls become women, there should be ceremony. When boys become men, there should be ceremony. When lovers join their lives, there should be a ceremony. When

The First 60 Days

there is a birth, there should be a ceremony. When there is death, there should be ceremony.

If people are members of a church, some events are marked by rituals, but Pam liked deeper more meaningful ceremonies, so she created them. Basically, sunrise was enough of a miracle to have a ceremony. All aspects of Life are miraculous if you choose to look at them in a sacred way. Thank you, Creator, Great Spirit for this day.

By the time of her 59th birthday, her parties had grown to several hundred attendees, with two music stages, one for electric music, and one for acoustic music. There were performances by many of our children's music groups, being everything from rock, punk, hip-hop and every other kind of music you can imagine. All music was welcome. Sometimes it got so loud that neighbors from a mile away would call and ask us to turn down the volume.

"Helpers" would arrive days, or a week in advance to "help" set up, and some would stay for a week after to "help" clean up. So now it was lasting 2 weeks and costing a couple of thousand dollars.

There was always dancing. It was always wonderful when the lesbian women would be in control of the music and dance. They really like to dance and have excellent taste in dance music. I'll never forget the looks of some of the straight women's faces when they saw Pam dancing with these women. They seemed to be both shocked and intrigued. It was like they were saying, "You mean you can dance like that?" There is such beauty in freely dancing.

So, by her 60th birthday, she, as well as our family were OVER the parties. Since her birthday was July 6, a lot of people started planning their 4th of July holidays around

Pam's party. She told me that for her 60th, she wanted me to come with her to a 7-day intensive Reiki training in New York. She didn't want a party any more, she wanted us both to become Reiki teachers so that we could work together. This was the beginning of her plan for our "retirement."

Our children told us that we could try to cancel the party, but that people would come anyway since they were so accustomed to attending. So, Pam sent out postcards, emails, and any other way she could, saying that her 60th birthday party was cancelled, and that she and I were leaving town and opting for room service, and motel sex. Somehow it worked! No one showed up, and that was the end of the parties. Pam and I did go to the 7-day training, and we also had room service and motel sex. It was the best birthday ever!!

May 26, 2022

I allowed myself a little extra sleep this morning. It felt good. I'm having difficulty writing this morning, given the news of another school shooting and the taking of innocent lives. There is something supremely tragic in this plague of violence in which we find ourselves. I try not to watch, or even listen to much news, but some things are even bigger than the grief that I'm feeling, and that's saying something.

I'm trying desperately to keep these posts about Pam's life, and our life together. I saw a news headline the other day saying Putin is reaping the whirlwind of his actions in Ukraine, and I can't help but think that we are experiencing the same. When a gun is drawn, or we go to war, the end results are always unpredictable.

Sadness and grief are the only sure things in both cases, and the difference between a good guy with a gun and a bad guy with a gun is mostly just a shift in perspective. I've seen both guys, and this is Memorial Day weekend, and I feel a deeper sense of grief than I thought was possible.

When Pam and I went to the 7-day training in New York, it was at a Buddhist Retreat Center near Woodstock. The facility was way up in the mountains, and there was no cell service, TV reception, or even radio reception, so for the entire week, there were no outside distractions. If our children needed to contact us, they could call the landline in the office, and the staff would get us in an emergency.

We had class all day, and then gathered in the evening after dinner for practice, often until late. There were about 40 people in the class, and we had 3 teachers, Michael, Laurelle, and William Rand. It was a wonderful experience, and we

The First 60 Days

grew both intellectually and spiritually through that class and met many interesting and colorful people there. It was 2005, and the first time that I ever considered the pain and fear that my parents, Pam, and my Loved ones must have suffered when I was in Vietnam. I was so consumed with my own experience that it had not occurred to me that they were suffering heavily as well.

In one of the meetings there was a woman whose son was being deployed to Iraq/Afghanistan. As I watched and listened to her describing her fear for her son and the desperation in her voice, it struck me full force. Oh my God....what they must have quietly suffered. Never exposing me to their fears and allowing me to process my own. How could I possibly have been so self-centered that it took this long to see that? I came to a deep understanding that in war, nobody gets out untouched. Even those who have "bone spurs" and avoid service and participation are affected in the end.

When the 7-day class ended, and we went down to the motel in Albany to sleep before the early morning flight home, the stark awareness of all the TVs and constant bombardment of news and "entertainment" was overwhelming. It was impossible to avoid. In the lobby, in the dining room, in the bar, in the service plaza on the highway, in the airport, everywhere. It wasn't pleasant.

Often Pam and I would take what we called a "media fast" during which time we would consciously avoid all forms of media input. It never is perfect, but it can put some things in perspective.

On the way back to the motel, we were riding with Michael, Laurelle, and William, and we stopped in Woodstock to get lunch. During lunch, William casually said to us that he was going to Hawaii for a while and that we should come visit while he was there. We said that he shouldn't say something like that to us, because we just might show up. He enthusiastically encouraged us to come.

We pondered it for some time, talking about how nice it would be to go back to our old place and see our landlady and friends on the Big Island while we were there. So, plans were laid for us to go back to Hawaii for the first time in over 20 years. We contacted Jackie, our landlady who was overjoyed that we might visit the Big Island, and she would pick us up at the Kona airport and we could stay in our old house.

The flight is not a particularly enjoyable thing, and is taxing on the body, but we got there. Jackie was a wonderful host and had a dinner party with quite a few of our old friends. It was bittersweet though because my old friend Norman, who I was really looking forward to seeing, had just passed away.

Kona itself had changed a good bit, with big box stores and a shopping district, but up on the mountain, in the coffee land, things were very much the same as when we lived there. But the plague of meth and crack had taken a toll on the people. One of our children's friends had OD'd, leaving his family devastated, and it was evident everywhere.

Of course, Jackie, always the political and social activist, was very active in efforts to rid the community of meth addiction and all the problems that follow it, but there was a sadness about it all. Jackie and our friends were wonderful, and Hawaii is still awesome and beautiful beyond description, and Pele still speaks there and will eventually wipe the tears away and cleanse the land.

Then we went to Maui and spent a week with William. Each island has its own energy, and Maui is very different than the Big Island. It is much softer, and there is sugar cane and pineapple culture in abundance. William's place was in Hana, a very small village on the far side of the island from the airport. He was a great host as well and took pleasure in showing us so much of the island.

When we left, we went to the summit of Haleakala, the big volcano mountain. What a spectacular place, and very easy to get sunburned in the thin air. By the time we got to the small airport we were hot, sweaty, and dirty.

My hair was tangled and so I unbraided it and started to comb it out and re-braid for the trip. I was frustrated and said to Pam offhandedly that I think I'm just going to cut my hair off. An older gentleman from the other side of the room came running over shouting, "No, no, no. If you're our age and still have hair like that, you have to represent!!" We laughed and talked with him for a while before boarding for the loooong flight back home.

It's difficult for me to believe that it's now been nearly another 20 years since we were there. Time. What to do with what's left. I don't know, but each day seems to keep happening, and I guess it will until it doesn't.

May 27, 2022

Normally, in the morning I just get up and start writing these posts as I have my lemon water. Today I picked up Pam's iPad and checked Facebook. The first thing I see is a post from my youngest son Willie D about him helping a pregnant deer that had been hit by a car.

He had taken the time to stop, get out, and do what he could to comfort the beautiful creature, and at least get her out of the road to prevent further damage. He checked her legs to see if they were broken and calmed her down. Events like this make me proud, happy, and hopeful.

I don't know where this crazy world is headed, but I see great wonder and hope in the actions of the children, and all my children are grown men now. I can get lost in my current situation of loneliness, sadness, and depression at the loss of Pam, and the inhumanity of war and violence, and then something like this happens to make me realize there are such good people here in balance to the daily insanity that is the "news." As Mr. Rogers said, "In times of tragedy, always look for the helpers."

After the 7-day Reiki training, we did begin to teach Reiki classes as well as Breathwork classes, and we loved it. Being able to work together and see the effects on people's lives just made our lives better, and better.

When, through a series of events, the little cabin next door to us became available, I told Pam that I thought that we should buy it and open a teaching space so that we could teach our classes right here instead of having to go through all the planning and coordination that it took to teach classes in so many different towns.

Waaaay back in 1987 at the Harmonic Convergence, Pam had mentioned that the little cabin and surrounding property would make a good teaching place. Now, in 2007, we had managed to pay off our mortgage, and all of our credit cards, and we were debt free. Pam would often say that all of our dreams had come true.

Spirit had just come to me and said, "Remember that teaching center that you wanted to build, well now it's time." Pam absolutely freaked out and said emphatically, "No! Donald T. we are 65 years old, and debt free with our home and small farm, and happy. I don't want to get another mortgage now and start all over."

But Spirit kept coming in and saying, "You need to do this." After a while, she said that she could begin to see it, and maybe we should check with the bank to see if we could qualify and get a loan to purchase it. In 2008, there was the financial crash, and so she was privately hoping that we could not get financing.

Sure enough, we went to our local Wells Fargo to apply for a home loan, and basically were told that the crash was so intense that they didn't have the money to lend. Pam was relieved. Then a neighbor suggested that we go to the small local bank and apply there. She said all the wealthy people bank there, and they should have resources.

We went to the little bank and talked to a wonderful lady, who listened while Pam explained what we wanted to do and gave all the embarrassing details of our hippie financial situation. She said, "I think this is a fabulous idea, and it's such a small loan we can keep it in house and service the loan from here. If I wasn't going to the beach, we could close in 2 weeks, but it will have to be 3 weeks." And it was done.

The First 60 Days

We now we were in debt again, but we had some additional property, and a little run down cabin to work on. We called it Heartspace, and it was the next phase in our retirement plan. There was a LOT of work to be done on the cabin to get it functional, so I started work on it.

An old friend and Vietnam vet buddy of mine stopped by. He was recovering from 20 years as a crack addict, and had been in construction work his whole life, and he said he could use a project to help him with his recovery, and I needed assistance, so we began work in earnest, along with my son Buddy.

It turned out to be a much more difficult project than I had anticipated. I thought that we could just do some small repairs, paint it, and start teaching. Not so. The more we demolished, the more we found that had to be replaced. Soon we had pretty much torn it down to the frame, and started all over again, all the while borrowing more money to do the renovation.

It was really hot and humid that summer, and at the end of one particularly difficult day, as we trudged up the hill to our home for dinner, we were totally wet with sweat, and dirty, and exhausted. I said to my friend, "Why are 65 year old men doing this to ourselves?" and without missing a step he replied, "So we can be 75 year old men doing this." In all, it took about 5 years to "complete" the renovation, and we had a grand opening for Heartspace.

It wasn't finished by any means, but we had set a date. The day before the opening ceremony, it started to rain. And it rained. And it rained. People had come for the opening from as far away as Arizona, Kentucky, Minnesota and more.

There was not enough parking at Heartspace, so a neighbor had agreed to let us park cars in her field. We shuttled people down all day in the rain. There were a couple of hundred participants, and it was a soggy day. At some point late in the afternoon, I was wet through and through, muddy, tired, and wished it would all just end.

After we squeezed 120 people upstairs in a teaching room that was designed for max of 25, and played some music, as the rain raged on, it was finally over....not quite. Up in the parking field, the rain had been so heavy, and the ground so saturated, that many of the cars had just sunk into the ground and at 11 at night in the pouring rain, I was pulling people out of the mud with my little 4-wheel drive truck.

FINALLY, the last of the participants was free and, on their way, and it was probably 1 in the morning. I was done, but that was opening day. Instead of a grand opening, it was more like a water christening.

After a few more years, we finally had it up and running, but retirement seemed farther away than ever. We were more in debt than we had ever been. Now we were in our early 70's. But Heartspace began to work. We started to have classes on the weekends, and concerts about once a month. The classes were absolutely wonderful. Heartspace was a truly healing place. The energy was amazing. It looked like we were finally going to be able to fulfill our idea of retirement and teach and play music together. It was working. Then, in August of 2019, Pam was diagnosed with breast cancer.

May 28, 2022

Pam did not have much faith in the Western medical system. We didn't really have a doctor or go to see one regularly until we were about 70 years old. I don't think she would have seen a doctor at all if I hadn't been insistent. I felt that since we were now on Medicare, we should find a doctor, get a yearly physical, a blood panel, and get a baseline for our current state of health.

She didn't actually care but agreed that if she could find a doctor that she was comfortable with, she would go. It took a while, but finally she found a woman doctor who was a licensed medical doctor, but also familiar with herbs and alternative medical treatments. They became good friends immediately, and we began getting yearly exams. Getting the bloodwork was really good, as we found some things that were out of balance, and we were able to correct them with dietary changes, and supplements.

The doctor wanted Pam to get a mammogram, because she had never had one. Pam didn't want to submit to that procedure, so they settled on a thermogram, which Pam agreed to. The day she got the thermogram, we were preparing to leave for a trip to Sedona to sing at the International Reiki Retreat the next day.

Within an hour of the procedure, Pam got a phone call from the doctor saying that there were highly irregular results in the thermogram, and she wanted her to get an actual mammogram as quickly as possible. Pam told her there was no way, that we were leaving the next day for a week in Sedona. The doctor insisted that she get one as soon as she got back, so she made an appointment for the day after our return.

The tone of her voice, and the urgency with which she wanted these additional tests were unsettling to say the least. When we got back, we went the next day to the imaging facility to get the mammogram. As soon as it was over, they said they needed to do a sonogram.

It was getting weirder. They let me be in the room while they were doing this procedure, so I could see the display. They didn't tell us the results there, but I could see the black areas in the images. There was a terrible sinking feeling in my stomach.

The radiologist came out and talked to Pam and told her that they thought it was breast cancer, but they needed to run some more tests to be sure. The next one was some kind of ct scan with dye injected. She almost stopped everything then.

She didn't want the dye injections, but the technicians said that they could not do the scan without it. So, she reluctantly submitted. This test confirmed that it was cancer. As soon as they said the word "cancer," everything in our world changed.

All plans were put on hold, and all of our attention was focused on Pam and her healing process, whatever that looked like. She didn't want to tell anyone of the diagnosis, not even the children. She said she didn't want anyone focused on the disease instead of the cure.

After some talk, we agreed that we needed to at least let our children know. I cannot tell you how difficult it was to tell our children that Pam had been diagnosed with cancer. She would never acknowledge that she had cancer, only that she had been diagnosed with cancer. She said she didn't want to give it that much power.

So more detailed scans were ordered, and appointments with a breast surgeon to discuss treatment options. We were now in the system. Then began the visits to the Cancer Center. The surgeon was a wonderful woman who walked into the treatment room, introduced herself, and proceeded to throw the charts on the table and said, "We're not going to discuss breast cancer today, because the scans indicated some more serious issues that need to be dealt with first.

The radiologist observed some spots on your liver, and a possible aneurysm on the thoracic artery. Right now, the breast cancer is very small, and is the least of the issues." Now we're off to more scans, biopsies, and tests.

A visit to the cardiac surgeon to discuss the aneurysm. The cardiac guy said that it wasn't an aneurysm, but that we could look at it again in a couple of years. Whew! One down.

After close examination by the liver people, whoever they are, it was decided that the spots on her liver were just fatty deposits and may have been there since childhood. Whew! Two down.

Back to the breast surgeon who said a lumpectomy should take care of the breast cancer because it was very small, and not invasive. So, more scans, and placing of little pieces of marker metal in the location of the actual cancer.

All of this had completely taken over our lives. Nothing else was getting done. The actual surgery was in December of 2019, BUT, when the results came back, they had not gotten clean margins, and wanted to do further surgery, and Pam was to get radiation treatments. At this point she said it was enough.

She said she wanted to work with a medical nutritionist that she was familiar with and had referred quite a few of her own clients to, and they had positive results. The breast surgeon actually agreed with Pam and said to work with the nutritionist for a year and then come back, and if the cancer was still present, we could try the surgery.

The nutritionist was fabulous, and Pam went on a radical diet and lifestyle change. It wasn't easy, but she was committed. A year later, when we went back to the breast surgeon, which required whole body scans, there was no sign of cancer in her body. Hallelujah!!

They still wanted her to do the radiation treatments, and take estrogen blockers, which she refused. The next year's examination gave us the 2 year clear diagnosis.

They still had her come see an oncologist to encourage her to do the radiation and take the blockers, but she was adamant that she would not do either of those things.

So, at some point in that time period, we started teaching again, and doing breath work intensive weekends. By the time of the second year clear, Heartspace was working well. We were teaching at least two weekends a month, usually a monthly concert, and Pam's private practice was active again.

Then COVID hit. Everything shut down. No classes, no concerts, and no in-person clients. Pam felt that with the stresses of the cancer treatment, and tests, that she was in a vulnerable state, so, for the next year and a half, she never went even as far as the mailbox. She did do her 2-mile walks when she was pretty sure she wouldn't run into anyone.

I was the only one to go out. I still had a few active computer clients, and somebody had to do the shopping.

In the beginning, I would come back from town, take off all my clothes on the porch, go immediately to the shower, and clothes went into the washer. Anything coming in the house was sanitized. People we knew were dying and some were becoming extremely ill and hospitalized, so we took this very seriously, and did all we could to protect Pam. When the pandemic began, Pam wanted to do something to help comfort people during this terrible time, so she re-started her Porch of Peace live broadcasts on Facebook.

Even while she was ill, she continued to broadcast every Tuesday evening. So many people from all over the world responded to her efforts with messages of how the broadcast was helping them through the pandemic. She continued to do these until shortly before her passing.

From the "control room," I was always in awe of how the words seem to flow from her to give comfort to so many people. I am blessed and thankful to have been in her presence for the time we had. She was, and is, a gift.

May 29, 2022

I began this series of posts on the morning of February 23, 2022. The morning when everything about my life had changed. It was a day of shock, disorientation, disbelief and complete loss of direction and any sense of self identity. The enormous level of response from all of you who found comfort and consolation through Pam and Pam's work, created a need, desire and indeed a driving compulsion in me to start writing to answer as many of your questions as possible.

What started out as a simple response on an unfamiliar social platform grew into something beyond whatever expectations I had. This is my 60th post about Pam's life, and our life together. It started with her death, and with this post, that part of the experience will be complete.

I'm going to tell you about that night, and the events leading into the morning/mourning process that began then and I guess will continue as long as my physical body remains in this three-dimensional world.

This doesn't mean that I will quit posting. I believe there are many more stories to tell, and lessons that we have learned that need to be conveyed in some form or another. I was speaking with two of her closest friends, and two of the original 7 women who did the women's empowerment weekends, and the subject of "Witness" came up. "Sacred Witness."

There are situations and events in my life that I have been privileged to witness. It's these things that I have been writing about. These are not things that I have made up or invented, but things that I have personally witnessed. I think that the way the world appears to be spinning out of control, it is important that we speak with authority about what we perceive as Truth, in what we have witnessed.

Not just me, but everybody. If we don't do that, things just continue to get worse. I never intended to write about segregation, civil rights, women's rights, LGBTQ rights, political issues, religious issues, war, PTSD or any of those things. They just come out, without any plan on my part. But all of this and much more were foundational parts and important components of mine and Pam's relationship.

Without bearing witness to these things that were so important to her, our story would be sadly incomplete. So, I did, and am.

Oddly, the Facebook platform, and your participation as a community has given me a way to speak of these things in a whole new way for me. It is not my intention to offend anyone or hurt anyone's feelings in any way. All I want to do is act as a sacred witness.

The day of February 22 began like many of the days before, with a thankful waking up with Pam, and a morning snuggle before getting up and fixing breakfast. I had a small amount of work to do that day, and we had two friends visiting, so they were all going to ride with me, and after my work we went and did the obligatory weekly grocery shopping stops and even hit the bakery for a treat. The day was exceptionally wonderful.

When we got home, and began to prepare the evening meal, Pam went to "dance" on her rebounder. She had been having issues and some leg pain from varicose veins, and the rebounder exercises and walking helped to relieve them.

She was in really good spirits, laughing and occasionally breaking out into song or chants. She stepped off of the rebounder to get a drink of water, when all of a sudden, she grabbed her chest and said, "Ouch, my chest hurts," and then she said, "I can't breathe." Our two friends and I jumped up and supported her, and she just went limp. We lowered her to the floor and called 911. She was already unconscious. 3 seconds. 3 seconds is all it took for her to go from laughing and dancing, to gone.

No warning, no gradual slipping away, just gone. I knew then, but didn't want to admit that she had left, so there was the dance with the first responders, and ambulance. The initial first responder to appear was a friend. He was one of the young people that we used to party with and play music for. I recognized him behind his mask.

She was gasping, and I kept encouraging her to breathe. What I didn't know then, but found out later, was that she was not breathing at all. The faces of the ambulance crew were not encouraging. They would take measurements of heartbeat, oxygen levels and I could hear them say, "This is not good."

So, they put her on a stretcher and took her to the ambulance, and away to the hospital. We live about 20 miles from the hospital, and I tried to follow them as closely as possible, but they were going too fast. Carolyn, my friend from Buffalo was with me on that ride.

We found the emergency room, and were told to wait, that she was being processed. The first person to come talk to me told me that they thought it was a heart attack, but they needed to do more tests, and they would move her to the intensive care unit and I would be able to see her soon.

I was busy texting our children and her brother to let them know that she was in the hospital, and they were working on her. By midnight, the actual cardiac surgeon came to speak with me. He came straight to the point. He was kind, but clear. Her brain had been without oxygen for over an hour.

The ambulance crew had given her CPR all the way to the hospital, and the emergency room crew had continued to give her CPR, but her heart had never started again on its own. He explained that what they thought was a heart attack was in fact a thoracic arterial dissection, leading to an aneurysm. In plain language, a small split had developed in her artery, allowing blood to get between the layers, leading to a bubble on the outer layer which ruptured.

He said that it could not have been diagnosed, could happen to anyone at any time, and it was unsurvivable. He was sorry. He said they could repair the artery, but that because of the brain damage......I stopped him.

I said she was very clear with me and the children that she did not want to be on a vent or kept alive by artificial means. He was relieved and said that they would move her to a private room. They had her on a vent, and had somehow made her heart start beating by artificial means.

I asked if there was time to inform her family, and he said her heart could stop at any time, and knowing what they know now, they would not attempt to restart it. I immediately started texting the children and family that she would not make it through the night, and if they wanted to say goodbye, they needed to hurry up. It was now 2 in the morning. Willie and Jesse were able to get there in time.

Willie came from Raleigh after the first text. He made it just in time. After just a couple of minutes, Willie looked at all the equipment hooked up to her and said, "Pop, get this shit off of her." Jesse agreed, and I asked them to take it all away.

They did, and it only took a short while for the end. After the vent was removed, she began that gasping thing again, with long pauses in between gasps. We were holding her, kissing her, and thanking her for her presence in our lives. Willie leaned over to kiss her, and all of a sudden she took a long, vigorous inhale, and relaxed exhale. It was more than minute, and I came and leaned over and gave her a kiss, and again, she took a long, vigorous inhale, and a relaxed exhale. I allowed her final breath to wash over my face. Then there was no more. The attending nurse checked her and said she was gone. I said, "Are you sure, because I'm not leaving unless we're absolutely sure." She said that in 10 minutes another nurse would come and confirm her death. In that 10 minutes, I could see the color leave her face, and she began to feel cold. When the next nurse came in, I knew it was over. A lifetime of joy and memories, and it was over.

So now you know. Maybe more than you wanted to. Beginning to end. The story is complete. There will be more stories, but this part of the journey is done. I Love you all.

Donald T. McMahon

There will be no memorial for her
Fashioned by the hand of man
No alabaster obelisk, nor polished granite stone
No Taj Mahal, nor gleaming pyramid
With magical words engraved to read
Of a life well lived and loved and accomplished accolades
Not even her name, or birth and death decrees
Laser etched or chiseled in perpetual precision
To remind generations of her footsteps or her breath
Instead, a circle of unhewn, found stones
Placed by her own hands in a quiet field
In a community of cedars and pines and a peach tree
No garlands nor florist arrangements
Instead, grasses and Creator placed wildflowers
A medicine wheel comforting us with directions
East, South, West, North, Above, Below
The guideposts of origins and destinations
The hOMeplace of the ancients and oracles
Commemorating HER life in eternal harmony with All Life
The Angels, ArchAngels, all relations and Christ dance here
Around the Circle, the Wheel within the Wheel
And as the rain washes the stones clean of her ashes
And she feeds the Earth as she fed us all
The Medicine wheel turns as Mother shivers
And Mary watches as the stones dissolve
And all is renewed, and resurrection is made manifest
Her voice is heard in the wind
Her face is seen in the clouds
The plants speak her name
There is no need for man to do anything

Epilogue

It has been more than a year since I began this process of writing the closing chapter of the story of Pam and Donald T. I'm older now. I'm more experienced than the former me. All of the firsts have slipped by. The first night. The first Mother's Day. The first birthdays. The first Christmas. The first wedding anniversary. The first solo performance. The first anniversary of her death. The first breath alone. All of those events now fade in the rear view mirror of a past life, and all of it gets fainter and smaller as the accelerator is pressed toward the floor and the scenes in the windows and windshield pass more quickly.

I know that to lose focus on the front windshield is dangerous, but I can't seem to shift my gaze from the retreating images in the rearview portal. I keep straining to see her face there, smiling and fading, and getting smaller as the journey continues. I have found that the "letting go" is by far the most difficult obstacle to navigate. And I must confess that I am failing in this part. I continue to hang on and refuse to let go because I can't believe in the finality of this. There are more stories to tell, and more work to do.

So, whether anyone ever reads these words or not, I will continue to write because as long as I continue to write, she remains present, and so do I. Every now and then I remove my eyes from the rearview and allow myself to look forward, and as frightening and disorienting as it is, I realize that I am in a new and foreign land without a map. It looks like the air is breathable in this new place, and I see some friendly faces, and maybe there will be some who like to sing and play music. Let me check the rearview one more time.......

Made in the USA
Las Vegas, NV
31 October 2023

80038920R00174